Science and Art Department

Catalogue of ship models and marine engineering

Science and Art Department

Catalogue of ship models and marine engineering

ISBN/EAN: 9783741172632

Manufactured in Europe, USA, Canada, Australia, Japa

Cover: Foto ©Andreas Hilbeck / pixelio.de

Manufactured and distributed by brebook publishing software
(www.brebook.com)

Science and Art Department

Catalogue of ship models and marine engineering

Science and Art Department
of the Committee of Council on Education.

CATALOGUE

OF

SHIP MODELS AND MARINE ENGINEERING

IN THE

SOUTH KENSINGTON MUSEUM.

WITH

CLASSIFIED TABLE OF CONTENTS, AND AN
ALPHABETICAL INDEX OF EXHIBITORS
AND SUBJECTS.

LONDON:
PRINTED BY GEORGE E. EYRE AND WILLIAM SPOTTISWOODE,
PRINTERS TO THE QUEEN'S MOST EXCELLENT MAJESTY.
FOR HER MAJESTY'S STATIONERY OFFICE.
1878.

Price One Shilling and Sixpence.

SCIENCE AND ART DEPARTMENT OF THE COMMITTEE OF COUNCIL ON EDUCATION,

SOUTH KENSINGTON.

ESTABLISHED in connexion with the Board of Trade in March 1853 as a development of the Department of Practical Art, which in 1852 had been created for the re-organisation of Schools of Design. Placed under the direction of the Committee of Council on Education in 1856.

List of Presidents and Vice-Presidents.

Board of Trade.

1852. Rt. Hon. H. Labouchere, M.P.
„ Rt. Hon. J. W. Henley, M.P.
1853. Rt. Hon. Edward Cardwell, M.P.
1855. Rt. Hon. Lord Stanley of Alderley.

Committee of Council on Education.

1850. Rt. Hon. Earl Granville, K.G., Lord President.
„ Rt. Hon. W. E. Cowper, M.P., Vice-President.
1858. Most Hon. Marquess of Salisbury, K.G.
„ Rt. Hon. Sir C. B. Adderley, K.C.M.G., M.P.
1859. Rt. Hon. Earl Granville, K.G.

1859. Rt. Hon. Robert Lowe, M.P.
1864. Rt. Hon. H. A. Bruce, M.P., Vice-President.
1866. His Grace the Duke of Buckingham and Chandos.
„ Rt. Hon. H. T. Lowry Corry, M.P.
1867. His Grace the Duke of Marlborough, K.G.
„ Rt. Hon. Lord Robert Montagu, M.P.
1868. Most Hon. Marquess of Ripon, K.G.
„ Rt. Hon. W. E. Forster, M.P.
1873. Rt. Hon. Lord Aberdare.
„ Right Hon. W. E. Forster, M.P.
1874. His Grace the Duke of Richmond and Gordon, K.G., Lord President.
„ The Rt. Hon. the Viscount Sandon, M.P., Vice-President.

OFFICE HOURS, TEN TO FOUR.

GENERAL ADMINISTRATION.

Secretary.—Sir F. R. Sandford, C.B.
Assistant Secretary.—Norman MacLeod.
Chief Clerk.—G. Francis Duncombe.
First-class Clerks.—A. J. R. Trendell; Alan S. Cole; F. R. Fowke; Alfred S. Bury.
Second-class Clerks.—J. B. Rundell; H. W. Williams; E. Belshaw.; G. G. Millard; A. F. E. Torrens; O. J. Dullea.
Postal Clerk.—W. Burtt.
Clerk of Accounts.—T. A. Bowler.
Book-keeper.—E. Harris.

GENERAL STORES.

Storekeeper.—W. G. Groser. *Deputy.*—H. Lloyd.
Clerks.—J. Smith; F. Walters.

SCIENCE DIVISION.

Director.—Lieut.-Col. Donnelly, R.E.
Occasional Inspectors.—F. J. Sidney, LL.D. Capt. Harris, E.I.C. (*Navigation*).
Official Examiner.—G. C. T. Bartley.
Assistant Professional Examiner.—T. Healey.

Professional Examiners for Science.

Subject.
I.—Practical, plane, and solid Geometry.—Lieut. G. S. Clarke, R. E.
II.—Machine Construction and Drawing.—W. C. Unwin, B.Sc.
III.—BuildingConstruction.—MajorSeddon, R.E.
IV.—Naval Architecture.—W.E. Baskcomb.
V.—Pure Mathematics.—C. W. Merrifield, F.R.S.; Rev. J. F. Twisden, M.A.; T. Savage, M.A.
VI.—Theoretical Mechanics.—Rev. John F. Twisden, M.A.
VII.—Applied Mechanics.—T. M. Goodeve, M.A.
VIII.—Acoustics, Light and Heat.—J. Tyndall, LL.D., F.R.S.; F. Guthrie, F.R.S.
IX.—Magnetism and Electricity.—J. Tyndall, LL.D., F.R.S.; H. Debus, F.R.S.
X.—Inorganic Chemistry.—E. Frankland, D.C.L., Ph.D., F.R.S.; H. E. Roscoe, B.A., Ph.D., F.R.S.

XI.—Organic Chemistry.—E. Frankland, D.C.L., Ph.D., F.R.S.; H. E. Roscoe, B.A., Ph.D., F.R.S.
XII.—Geology.—H. W. Bristow, F.R.S.
XIII.—Mineralogy.—W. W. Smyth, M.A., F.R.S.
XIV.—Animal Physiology.—T. H. Huxley, LL.D., Sec. R.S.; M. Foster, M.D., F.R.S.
XV.—Elementary Botany.—W. T. T. Dyer, M.A., B.Sc., F.L.S.
XVI.—{ General Biology.—T. H. Huxley,
XVII.—{ LL.D., Sec. R.S.; M. Foster, M.D., F.R.S.; W. T. T. Dyer, M.A., B.Sc., F.L.S.
XVIII.—Mining.—W. W. Smyth, M.A., F.R.S.
XIX.—Metallurgy.—J. Percy, M.D., F.R.S.
XX.—Navigation.—J. Woolley, LL.D.
XXI.—Nautical Astronomy.—J. Woolley, LL.D.
XXII.—Steam.—T. M. Goodeve, M.A.
XXIII.—{ Physical Geography.—D. T. Ansted, M.A., F.R.S. Physiography.—J. Norman Lockyer, F.R.S.; J. W. Judd, F.R.S.
XXIV.—Principles of Agriculture, H. Tanner, F.C.S.

ART DIVISION.

Director.—E. J. Poynter, R.A.
Assistant Director.—H. A. Bowler.
Occasional Inspectors.—S. A. Hart, R.A.; Eyre Crowe, A.R.A.; F. B. Barwell; W. B. Scott.
Official Examiner.—T. Chesman, B.A., LL.B.
Professional Examiners, 1877.—F. R. Pickersgill, R.A.; W. F. Yeames, A.R.A.; J. E. Hodgson, A.R.A.; J. E. Boehm; Wm. Morris; J. Stevenson; J. Marshall, F.R.S., F.R.C.S.; E. J. Poynter, R.A.; and H. A. Bowler.
Assistant Professional Examiner.—J. A. D. Campbell.
Occasional Examiners.—G. M. Atkinson; G. R. Redgrave.

Inspectors of Local Schools of Science and Art.—R. G. Wylde; J. F. Iselin, M.A.; E. P. Bartlett; Capt. W. de W. Abney, R.E., F.R.S.

Organising Master of Science and Art Classes.—J. C. Buckmaster, F.C.S.

A

NATIONAL ART TRAINING SCHOOL.

Principal.—E. J. Poynter, R.A.
Head Master.—J. Sparkes.
Registrar.—R. W. Herman.
Mechanical and Architectural Drawing.—H. B. Hagreen.
Geometry and Perspective.—E. S. Burchett.
Painting, Freehand Drawing of Ornament,&c., the Figure and Anatomy and Ornamental Design.—J. Sparkes; C. P. Slocombe; T. Clack, and F. M. Miller.
Modelling.—Jules Dalou; F. M. Miller.
Lady Superintendent of Female Classes.—Miss Truelock.
Instructors.—Mrs. S. E. Casabianca; Miss Channon.
Occasional Lecturers.—E. Bellamy, F.R.C.S., *Anatomy*; Dr. Zerffi, *Historic Ornament*; R. W. Herman, *Principles of Ornamental Construction*; F. W. Moody, *The Figure.*
Teacher of Etching Class.—A. Legros.
Teacher of Wood Engraving Class.—C. Roberts.

SOUTH KENSINGTON MUSEUM.

Director.—P. Cuncliffe Owen,C.B., temp.absent.
Acting Director.—R. A. Thompson.
Assistant Directors.—Major E. R. Festing, R.E.; Col. Sir H. B. Sandford (Acting).
Director of New Buildings.—Major-Gen. Scott, C.B., F.R.S.
Instructor in Decorative Art and Decorative Artist.—F. W. Moody.
Decorative Artist.—R. Townroe.
Museum Keeper (Art Collections).—G. Wallis.
Museum Keeper (National Art Library).—R. H. Soden Smith, M.A., Trinity College, Dublin, F.S.A.
Museum Keeper (Educational Library and Collection).—A. C. King, F.S.A.
Assistant Museum Keepers.—W. Matchwick, F.L.S.; H. Sandham; R. Laskey; C. B. Worsnop; R. F. Sketchley, B.A., Exeter College, Oxford; H. E. Acton; J. W. Appell, Ph.D.; J. Barrett, B.A.; C. H. Derby, B.A.
Museum Clerks.—M. Webb, H. M. Cundall; L. Finding.
Special and Technical Assistants.—W. E. Streatfeild; A. Reid; H. Vernon; A. Masson; F. Coles; W. G. Johnson; S. Cowper; O. Scott.
Superintendent for Examples and Publications.—J. Cundall.

BETHNAL GREEN BRANCH OF THE SOUTH KENSINGTON MUSEUM.

(Opened on June 24, 1872.)

GEOLOGICAL SURVEY.

Director-General.—A. C. Ramsay, LL.D., F.R.S.
Director for England and Wales.—H. W. Bristow, F.R.S.
Director for Ireland.—E. Hull, M.A., F.R.S.
Director for Scotland.—A. Geikie, LL.D., F.R.S.
Naturalist.—T. H. Huxley, LL.D., Sec.R.S.
Palæontologist.—R. Etheridge, F.R.S.

ROYAL SCHOOL OF MINES AND MUSEUM OF PRACTICAL GEOLOGY.

Director of Museum of Practical Geology.—A. C. Ramsay, LL.D., F.R.S.
Keeper of Mining Records.—Robert Hunt, F.R.S.
Assistants.—Richard Meade; James B. Jordan.
Registrar, Curator, and Librarian.—T. Reeks.
Assistant Librarian.—T. Newton.
Assistant Curator.—A. Pringle.

| PROFESSORS.

Chemistry.—Edward Frankland, D.C.L., Ph.D., F.R.S.
Natural History.—T. H. Huxley, LL.D.,Sec.R.S.
Physics.—F. Guthrie, B.A., Ph.D., F.R.S.
Applied Mechanics.—T. M. Goodeve, M.A.
Metallurgy.—J. Percy, M.D., F.R.S.
Geology.—J. W. Judd, F.R.S.
Mining and Mineralogy.—W. W. Smyth, M.A., F.R.S.
Mechanical Drawing.—Rev. J. H. Edgar, M.A.
Museum open every week-day but Friday, and on Saturdays and Mondays from 10 a.m. till 10 p.m., except from the 10th of August to the 10th of September.

EDINBURGH MUSEUM OF SCIENCE AND ART.

Director.—Professor T. C. Archer, F.R.S.E.
Keeper of Natural History Collections.—Prof. R. H. Traquair, M.D.
Curator.—Alexander Galletly.
Assistant in Natural History Museum.—J. Gibson.
Assistant in Industrial Museum.—W. Clark.
Clerks.—C. N. B. Muston; T. Stock.

ROYAL COLLEGE OF SCIENCE, DUBLIN.

Dean of Faculty.—E. Hull, M.A., F.R.S.
Secretary.—F. J. Sidney, LL.D.
Curator of Museum.—A. Gages.
Clerk.—G. C. Penny.

PROFESSORS.

Physics.—W. F. Barrett, F.C.S.
Chemistry.—R. Galloway, F.C.S.
Geology.—E. Hull, M.A., F.R.S.
Applied Mathematics.—H. Hennessy, F.R.S.
Botany.—W. R. McNab, M.D.
Zoology.—A. Leith Adams, M.B., F.R.S.
Descriptive Geometry and Drawing.—Thomas F. Pigot, C.E.
Mining and Mineralogy.—J. P. O'Reilly, C.E.
Demonstrator in Palæontology.—W. H. Baily, F.L.S.
Assistant Chemist.—W. Plunkett.
Assistant Physicist.—A. E. Porte.

SCIENCE AND ART MUSEUM, DUBLIN,

with the

NATIONAL LIBRARY, SCHOOL OF ART, AND BOTANICAL GARDENS.

(*Staff under Re-organisation.*)

ZOOLOGICAL GARDENS, DUBLIN.

Secretary.—Rev. S. Haughton, M.D., D.C.L., F.T.C.D., F.R.S.

CATALOGUE OF THE COLLECTION

OF

Ship Models and Marine Engineering in the South Kensington Museum.

PREFACE.

THE present collection of Models of ships of the Mercantile Marine, and Ships of War, has been acquired by loans and gifts from private sources to the South Kensington Museum, since the formation in 1864 of a collection of Ship Models illustrating naval architecture and marine engineering.

On the removal to Greenwich in 1873 of the collection of naval models belonging to the Admiralty it was determined to continue, as part of the collections of the South Kensington Museum, an exhibition of the Models of ships and tackle in connexion with them, acquired from time to time by the Science and Art Department of the Committee of Council on Education; these now form a tolerably complete series.

To the Models of ships are added Models and Drawings of steam-engines applied to the propulsion of ships by screw propellers or paddle wheels, also of marine steam boilers, engine and boiler accessories, as well as various other illustrations of steamship machinery in general.

A valuable nucleus for the study of the science of marine architecture and engineering thus exists, and now forms a permanent and extensive portion of the National Collections of the Museum.

Great assistance has been received from many private ship-building and engineering firms in forming the present collection of Marine Models for public instruction in London.

A 2

The annexed account of the history of the "Navy Office" or present Admiralty, taken from the preface to the catalogue of the models formerly exhibited by the Admiralty in the South Kensington Museum, may perhaps be found interesting.

H. SANDHAM.

November, 1877.

The following short historical sketch of the Navy Office, extracted chiefly from the 5th Report of the Commissioners of Inquiry, dated 14th February 1788, (page 25) contains some very interesting information :—

"The records of the office do not furnish us with any information further back than July 1660, but we understand that the first establishment of Royal Navy office was in the reign of King Henry VIII., who appointed certain officers, under the title of principal officers of his navy, to manage the civil branches thereof, under the Lord High Admiral ; but these officers had no positive instructions for their guidance in the execution of their duty until the reign of Edward VI., when certain ordinances were issued for the conduct of the officers entrusted with the management of the marine affairs, which ordinances form the basis of all later instructions given for the conduct of the officers to whom the management of the civil branches of the Navy was committed. The officers at that time appointed to this duty were the Vice-Admiral of the Fleet, the Master of the Ordnance, the Surveyor of Marine Causes, the Treasurer, the Controller, the General Surveyor of the Victualling, the Clerk of the Ships, and the Clerk of the Stores, who were directed to meet once a week at the office on Tower Hill, to consult together for the good order of the Navy, and to report their proceedings once a month to the High Admiral ; particular duties were also assigned to each member.

"The affairs of the Navy appear to have continued under the management of such officers until the time of King James I., who, in the sixteenth year of his reign, issued a commission under the great seal to Sir Thomas Smith and others, to inquire into the frauds and abuses which had been committed in the Navy, with power to remedy the same, and to manage, settle, and put the officers of the Navy into a right course. This commission was determined upon the demise of King James I. in 1625, when his successor, King Charles I., issued a new commission to the same persons. By this commission the offices of the controller and surveyor were suspended during its continuance, and the same continued in force until the year 1628, when it was made void by a new commission, restoring the management of the affairs of the

Navy to the ancient principal officers established in the reign of King Edward VI. ; but between this time and breaking out of the Civil War several commissions appear to have been issued for regulating and settling the affairs of the Navy, during the continuance of which the functions of the original principal officers were always suspended.

"Upon the restoration of King Charles II. his Majesty constituted a Navy Board, by commission under the great seal, consisting of the Treasurer, Controller, Surveyor, and Clerk of the Navy, who were styled principal officers, to whom, on the 4th July 1660, three commissioners were added, to assist the said principal officers in the management of the affairs of the Navy.

"In January 1661 the Duke of York (then Lord High Admiral) established certain instructions now in use (1778) for the conduct of the four principal officers ; the other three being commissioners at large, had no particular line of duty allotted to them until the year 1666, when one of them was directed to take upon him so much of the controller's duty as related to the examination and control of the treasurer's accounts; another that part relating to victualling accounts; and in the year 1671, the third commissioner had that part of the controller's duty which related to the examination and control of the storekeeper's accounts, assigned to him, which, with the addition of one commissioner at large, is the present (1778) arrangement of the Navy Board."

In consequence of the great increase of the Navy, these arrangements were found incomplete and insufficient to insure the strict investigation and examination of accounts, the direction and proper conduct of correspondence and supervision of stores ; instead of the commissioners presiding over separate departments, committees were formed, and the business divided so as to admit of competent officers in each branch, possessing time and opportunity, to examine, digest, and conduct the parts allotted to them. Under this idea, by Order in Council of 8th June 1796, the Navy Board was divided into the three following committees:—

A Committee of Correspondence.

A Committee of Accounts.

A Committee of Stores.

The controller to belong to and preside at every committee.

The designing, building, and repair of ships was in the hands of the surveyors, of whom at one time there were three, and generally two, under the presidency of the controller.

In the year 1796 the Board consisted of the following members, viz.:—Sir Andrew Snape Hamond, Bart., Controller ; Charles Hope, Esq., Deputy Controller; Sir John Henslowe and Sir W. Rule, Surveyors ; George Marsh, Esq., George Rogers, Esq., William Palmer, Esq., Sir William Bellingham, Bart., Harry Harwood, Esq., and Samuel Gambier, Esq.

The office of Deputy Controller was abolished in the year 1816. In the following year the Transport Board, created in 1793, was broken up, and a Transport Committee was formed at the Navy Board.

A surveyor was reduced in 1822, and a civil commissioner in the same year, leaving at the Board the following persons, viz. :— one Controller, two Surveyors, three Naval Officers, and three Civil Commissioners, in the whole nine, and thus employed :— Two at the Committee of Correspondence, two at the Committee of Accounts, two at the Committee of Stores, two at the Committee of Transport, with the controller at the head of each.

In 1832, during the presidence of Sir James Graham at the Board of Admiralty, the Navy Board was abolished, the civil affairs of the Navy being for the future conducted by the principal officers, under the direct control of the Board of Admiralty. At that time the department charged with the design and construction of ships consisted of a Surveyor (a naval officer) and two Assistant Surveyors. In 1857 this department was placed under a Controller (a naval officer), one Chief Constructor, and one Constructor, to which staff an Assistant Constructor was added in 1861. In 1864, by Order in Council, the constitution of the office was altered to a Controller, a Chief Constructor, and three Assistant Constructors.

The several Royal Dockyards were established as under :—

Deptford - - Early in the reign of Henry VIII. Closed April 1869.

Woolwich - Called by Camden the Mother Dockyard, in the reign of Henry VIII., about 1509. Closed October 1st, 1869.

Chatham - - In the reign of Queen Elizabeth on the site of the present gun wharf; removed to the present site about the year 1622.

Sheerness - - Established in the reign of Charles II., about 1661. The present dockyard and basins were completed about the year 1823.

Portsmouth - In the reign of Henry VIII. In 1666, a dry dock and the Commissioner's house were built; and in 1848 the steam factory and steam basin were formed.

Plymouth - Prior to 1691, the Master Shipwright and workmen were borne on board of a ship fitted for their reception; and in 1693, in the reign of William and Mary, the dockyard was completed. In the year 1824, the name was changed from Plymouth Dock to Devonport.

Milford - A temporary yard, prior to 1815, at which time it was removed to Pater Hobb's Point, and is now known as Pembroke Dockyard.

CLASSIFICATION

Of the Collection of SHIP MODELS and MARINE ENGINEER-
ING in the SOUTH KENSINGTON MUSEUM.

Class I.   Whole MODELS—rigged and unrigged—Repre-
              senting lines and forms of sailing ships and
              steam ships. Page 7.

Class II.   Half-block MODELS of sailing ships and steam
              ships, showing lines and forms. Page 22.

Class III.   MODELS of construction. Sailing ships and
              steam ships, wood and iron.—Keels, timbers,
              frames, beams, knees, &c. Sectional models.
              Page 34.

Class IV.   MODELS of fitments. Cabins and their fittings.
              Ports, skylights, hatchways, ladders, &c.—
              Ventilation of ships. Fire hearths (cooking),
              cabin stoves. Page 53.

Class V.   APPLIANCES used in ships. Capstans and
              windlasses. Tanks, pumps, &c. Anchors
              and chain cables, and gear connected with
              them. Page 56.

Class VI.   MASTS. Rigging, standing and running. Rope.
              Blocks. Sails. Page 60.

Class VII.   METHODS OF PROPULSION. Oars and sculls,
              sweeps. Steam engines and boilers. Screw
              propellers, paddle wheels, &c. Page 66.

Class VIII.   STEERING APPARATUS. Rudders, permanent
              and temporary. Steering gear of all kinds,
              manual and steam power. Page 80.

Class IX.   BOATS. Ships' boats. Life-boats and rafts. All
              kinds of boats and barges used for pleasure.
              Page 83.

Class X.   INSTRUMENTS FOR NAVIGATION. Compasses,
              logs, chronometers, sextants, &c. Barometers.
              Nautachometers, clinometers, &c. Signal
              flags and ships' lights. Page 91.

CATALOGUE.

CLASS I.

Whole Models—rigged and unrigged—showing Lines and Forms of Sailing Ships and Steam Ships.

1. WHOLE MODEL, full-rigged, of H.M.S. "RACOON," (on a $\frac{3}{16}$-in. scale), 22 guns, 400 horse-power.

> *Note.*—The "RACOON," 22 guns, 400 horse-power, length 200 ft. 1 in., breadth 40 ft. 4 in., depth 22 ft. 8 in., tonnage 1,467, was laid down at Chatham Yard in April 1856. Launched in April 1857. Designed by Surveyor's Department, Admiralty.

There were also built on the same lines the "CHALLENGER," at Woolwich in 1858, and the "CLIO," at Sheerness in 1858. The armament was as follows:

No.	Prs.	Weight.	Length.
		cwt.	ft. in.
20 -	- 8-in. -	- 60 -	- 8 10
2 -	- 68-pr. pivot -	- 95 -	- 10 0

22 Total. The complement of men was 280.

Lent by H.R.H. the Duke of Edinburgh. 1865.

2. WHOLE MODEL, full-rigged, of H.M.S. "NORTHUM-BERLAND," (iron), 26 guns, 1,350 horse-power, screw (on a $\frac{1}{2}$-in. scale). Length 400 ft., breadth 59 ft. 3½ in., depth 21 ft. 1 in., tonnage 6,621. Built (1865) by contract at Millwall, by the Millwall Iron Works and Shipbuilding Company. She was commenced by Messrs. C. J. Mare & Co., at their Yard at Millwall in October 1861. Designed by the Controller's Department, Admiralty.

There were also built on the same lines the " MINOTAUR " and " AGINCOURT."

The armament is—

	No.	Prs.	
Main deck	{ 4	- 300	- 12-ton guns.
	{ 18	- 100	- 6½ „
Upper „	- 4	- 100	- 6½ „

Total 26

Note.—This MODEL, showing three masts and 50 guns, was made before the masting and armament of the ship had been decided on. The ship now has five masts and 26 guns.

Lent by the Millwall Iron Works Company.   1865.

3. WHOLE MODEL, full-rigged, of H.M.S. " AJAX " (on a ¼-in. scale); 64 guns, tonnage 1,953. Laid down at Messrs. Randall's yard, on the Thames, in 1795, launched in 1798, burnt in 1807.

This model was constructed by the late Sir Joseph Sydney Yorke, Bart., between the years 1797 and 1808.

Presented by the Earl of Hardwicke.   1865.

4. WHOLE MODEL of a design for a Four-decked ship of war, " DUKE OF KENT," to carry 170 guns.

Proposed by Mr. Joseph Tucker in 1809, when Master Shipwright of Plymouth Dockyard.

Lent by Mr. J. S. Tucker.   1865.

See also Class III., p. 36, No. 8.

5. SERIES OF MODELS, presented in 1867, by Messrs. R. Napier & Sons, Glasgow, illustrating a system of proposals and plans for combined Turret and Broadside navies, by the late Vice-Admiral Edward Pellew Halsted, R.N.

The ships, designed by C. F. Henwood, Esq., Naval Architect, are fitted on the turret and iron tripod mast system of the late Captain Cowper P. Coles, R.N., C.B.

The guns proposed for the armament of these ships, are wholly constructed and rifled on the principle for heavy ordnance of Sir Joseph Whitworth, Bart. ; and are mounted upon the muzzle-pivoting gun carriages designed by Captain T. B. Heathorn, R.A.

See Whitworth projectiles, Class XI., No. 3, pp. 97, 98.

5a. WHOLE MODEL, full-rigged, of the proposed ship-of-war " DREADNOUGHT," classed as a first-rate. 7 Turrets.

Turrets　　　-　　　-　　　-　7
Number of guns in turrets　　- 14 of 9-inch calibre.
Number of broadside guns　　- 4 of 7-inch calibre.
　and　　　-　　　-　- 10 of 4-inch　　„
Tonnage, 10,764, builder's old measurement.
Nominal horse-power, 1,300.
Length of ship, 455 feet.　Breadth, 70 feet.
Depth, 28 feet.　Load draught, 26 feet 6 inches.
Designed May 1866.　Scale, ¼ inch to 1 foot.

Note.—The masts and rigging of this model illustrate the following conditions :—

　Foremast : shows the mast as it would appear when " prepared for action," and ship steaming head to wind.

Mainmast : represents the position of the yards and sails when " sailing close hauled."

Mizenmast : represents the yards squared and dressed, ship lying in harbour.

5b. WHOLE MODEL, full-rigged, of the proposed ship-of-war " ACTIVE," classed as a corvette or 6th-rate. 2 Turrets.

Turrets　　　-　　　-　　　- 2
Number of guns in turrets　　- 4 of 9-inch calibre.
Number of broadside guns　　- 10 of 7-inch　　„
Tonnage, 4,926, builder's old measurement.
Nominal horse-power, 1,000.
Length of ship, 367 feet 6 inches.　Breadth, 52 feet 6 inches.　Depth, 25 feet.
Load draught, 24 feet 6 inches.
Designed May 1866.　Scale, ¼ inch to 1 foot.

Note.—The yards on the masts of this model show the ship as "running before the wind."

5c. WHOLE MODEL, unrigged, of the proposed ship-of-war or ocean despatch vessel " VEDETTE," classed as an 8th-rate ship. 1 Turret.

Turret　　　-　　　-　　　- 1
Number of guns in turret　　- 2 of 9-inch calibre.
Number of broadside guns　　- 10 of 5½ inch　„
Tonnage, 3,648, builder's old measurement.
Displacement, 5,700 tons.
Nominal horse-power, 800.
Length of ship, 332 feet 6 inches.　Breadth, 47 feet 6 inches.　Depth, 23 feet.
Load draught, 22 feet 6 inches.
Designed May 1866.　Scale, ¼ inch to 1 foot.

The Models *a., b., c., d.,* presented by Messrs. R. Napier & Sons, Glasgow. 1867.
See Models, No. 8, pp. 23, 24; No. 14, p. 37; No. 18 p. 42; No. 3, p. 83; Nos. 16 and 17, p. 101.

6. WHOLE MODEL of a proposed armour-plated frigate with two batteries, carrying 6 heavy rifled guns in each, besides 28 broadside guns.
Length of ship, 444 feet.
Designed by Mr. George Turner, late Master Shipwright, Woolwich Dockyard.   Lent 1864.

7. WHOLE MODEL of a proposed armour-plated frigate, carrying a battery of 8 heavy rifled guns and 14 broadside guns. Length of ship, 330 feet.
Designed by Mr. George Turner, late Master Shipwright, Woolwich Dockyard.   Lent 1864.

8. WHOLE MODEL of a proposed armour - plated corvette, carrying a battery of 4 heavy rifled guns and 4 broadside guns Length of ship, 210 feet.
Designed by Mr. George Turner, late Master Shipwright, Woolwich Dockyard.   Lent 1864.

9. WHOLE MODEL of H.M.S. "CHESTER," 50 guns. Built at Chatham or Woolwich, about 1670.
Lent by Mr. J. Dafforne.   1869.
Note.—With this model are also exhibited the lower masts, yards and spars, bowsprit, and other rigging gear of the ship.

10. WHOLE MODEL, brig-rigged, of a proposed ironclad war vessel, with turret and battery combined, on a system proposed and designed by Mr. R. Dawson.
The Model represents a ship 316 feet long, 66 feet beam, 4,000 tons. Draught of water, 20 feet; freeboard, 16 feet.
Presented by Mr. R. Dawson.   1870.

11. WHOLE MODEL of an armour-plated frigate, illustrating Mr. R. Griffith's proposals for improved screw propulsion. The ship is fitted with a bow and stern screw propeller placed well under the ship, and working in circular tunnels.
Note.—The chief objects desired by this system for ship propulsion are :—Increase of speed, and economy of fuel. Protection to the screws. No vibration from the propellers. Reduction in size of engines and screws. Increased facility for manœuvring the vessel. In case of disablement to either screw, propelling power is available from the other.
Proposed by Mr. R. Griffiths in 1872, and lent by him.   1874.

12. WHOLE MODEL of the 74 gun French ship-of-war " LE SCEPTRE." Date about 1700–1750. Full-rigged. No sails.

Purchased from Mr. G. Broker. 1871.

13. WHOLE MODEL of the Trinity House paddle steam yacht "GALATEA." Tons 507 B.M. Nominal horse-power 200. Makers of the engines, Messrs. Laird, Brothers, Birkenhead. Launched in 1867. Built by Messrs. Caird and Company, Greenock.

Lent by the Corporation of the Trinity House. 1869.

14. WHOLE MODEL of the Turkish iron armour-clad screw frigates "OSMANEA," "AZIZEA," and " ORKHANEA." Length 293 ft., beam 36 ft., tonnage 4,222, builders' measurement, guns 42, nominal horse-power 900. Constructed for the Imperial Ottoman Government by R. Napier & Sons.

Presented by Messrs. R. Napier & Sons, Glasgow. 1867.

15. WHOLE MODEL of a design for an armour-plated war vessel, on the turret principle. Submitted to the Admiralty in 1862. Length 365 ft., breadth 60 ft., tons 6,300, horse-power 1,160, speed 15 knots, guns 22.

Lent by Messrs. Westwood & Baillie, Isle of Dogs, Poplar. 1865.

16. WHOLE MODEL of H.M.'s Indian relief, steam troopship "JUMNA." Built 1866, by Palmer's Shipbuilding Company, Limited, Newcastle. Length 365 ft., breadth 48 ft. 9 in., depth 42 ft., tonnage gross 4,174, horse-power 700 nominal, speed 14½ knots per hour. Scale 1-48th full size.

Lent by the Palmer's Shipbuilding Company, Limited, Newcastle-on-Tyne. 1874.

Note.—There were also built on the same lines, about the same time, the " MALABAR," by Messrs. Napier & Sons ; the " CROCODILE," by Messrs. Wigram ; the " SERAPIS," by the Thames Iron Shipbuilding Company ; and the "EU- " PHRATES," built of iron, 700 horse-power. A class of five to form a direct service for the transport of troops to and fro between England and India. Length of the " EUPHRATES " 360 ft., breadth 49 ft., draught 19 ft. forward, 21 ft. aft, tonnage 4,206, speed 14·718 knots. Built by contract by Messrs. Laird, Brothers. Laid down in May 1865, launched November 1866. Designed by the Controller's Department, Admiralty.

17. WHOLE MODEL of the mail screw steamer "MON-
" TANA," Liverpool and New York line. Built 1873, by
the Palmer's Shipbuilding Company, Limited. Length
412 ft., breadth 43½ ft., depth 42¾ ft., tonnage gross 4,320
horse-power 900 nominal, speed 15½ knots per hour. Scale
1-48th full size.
Lent by the Palmer's Shipbuilding Company,
Limited, Newcastle-on-Tyne.   1874.

18. WHOLE MODEL of the mail screw steamer "BRIN-
" DISI," Ancona and Alexandria line. Built by the
Palmer's Shipbuilding Company, Limited. Length 260 ft.,
breadth 28 ft., depth 21½ ft., tonnage gross 900, horse-
power 180 nominal, speed 13 knots per hour. Scale 1-48th
full size.
Lent by the Palmer's Shipbuilding Company,
Limited, Newcastle-on-Tyne.   1874.
See also Nos. 14 and 15, page 26.

19. Series of WHOLE MODELS representing various
paddle and screw steamships of war and commerce. Designed and built by Messrs. Laird Brothers, engineers and
shipbuilders, Birkenhead.   Lent 1873.

19. WHOLE MODEL of the armour-clad gun-boat "BAHIA."
Imperial Brazilian Government. Length 175 ft., breadth
35 ft., depth 11 ft., tons 1,008, draught 8 ft., horse-power 140.
Built 1865. Scale ¼ in. to 1 foot.

19. WHOLE MODEL of the armour-clad monitor "HEILIGER-
" LEE." Royal Dutch navy. Length 180 ft., breadth 44 ft.,
depth 11 ft. 6 in., tons 1,588, draught 9 ft., horse-power 140.
Built 1868. Scale ¼ in. to 1 foot.

19. WHOLE MODEL of the screw steam yacht "MORE VANE."
Length 57 ft. 5 in., breadth 11 ft., depth 5 ft. 4 in., tons 35,
draught 5 ft. 6 in., horse-power 15. Built 1869. Scale ¼ in.
to 1 foot.

19. WHOLE MODEL of screw steam barge, to carry a 12-pr.
howitzer-gun. Length 50 ft., breadth 11 ft., depth 4 ft. 9 in.,
tons 28, draught 3 ft., horse-power 10. Built 1867. Scale
½ in. to 1 foot.

19. WHOLE MODEL of screw steam yacht " LANCASHIRE
" WITCH." S. Platt, Esq., owner. Fitted with R. R. Bevis'
feathering screw propeller. Length 106 ft. 6 in., breadth
18 ft., depth 9 ft. 6 in., tons 165, draught 7 ft., horse-
power 35 ft. Built 1872. Scale ¼ in. to 1 foot.

19. WHOLE MODEL of the royal mail screw steamers, "SANTA
ROSA" and "COLOMBIA." Pacific Steam Navigation Company. Length 300 ft., breadth 32, depth 22 ft. 3 in., tons
2,150, draught 13 ft. 3 in., horse-power 400. Built 1872.
Scale ¼ in. to 1 ft.

19. WHOLE MODEL of the royal mail screw steamer "BRITANNIA." Pacific Steam Navigation Company. Length 399 ft., breadth 43 ft., depth 35 ft. 3 in., tons 3,700, draught 22 ft., horse-power 600. Built 1873. Scale ¼ in. to 1 ft.

See also Drawing, No. 68, page 132.

19. WHOLE MODEL of H.M.'s armour-clad turret ship "WIVERN." Length 220 ft., breadth 42 ft., depth 19 ft. 6 in., tons 1,827, draught 15 ft., horse-power 350. Built 1864. Scale ¼ in. to 1 ft.

Note.—The "WIVERN" (formerly "EL MONASSIR"), iron, shield ship, 4 guns, 350 horse-power, screw, rigged. Built by Messrs. Laird at Birkenhead, launched 1864. There was also built on the same lines the "SCORPION" (formerly "EL TOUSSON,") at Birkenhead at the same time. The armament of H.M.S. "WIVERN" is four 12-ton guns in revolving shields, upon the plan of the late Captain C. P. Coles, R.N., C.B.

19. WHOLE MODEL of the armour-clad turret ship "DE "STIER." Royal Dutch navy. Length 195 ft., breadth 38 ft., depth 19 ft., tons 1,312, draught 15 ft. 6 in., horse-power 350. Built 1868. Scale ¼ in. to 1 ft.

19. WHOLE MODEL of the light-draught paddle steamer "CRANBORNE," for Indian river steam navigation. Length 213 ft., breadth 28 ft., depth 7 ft. 7 in., tons 819, draught 3 ft. 6 in., horse-power 150. Built 1866. Scale ¼ in. to 1 ft.

19. WHOLE MODEL of a light-draught paddle steamer for Indian river navigation. Length 90 ft., breadth 15 ft., depth 4 ft., tons 97, draught 2 ft. 2 in., horse-power 30. Built 1871. Scale ¼ in. to 1 ft.

The above 11 models lent by Messrs. Laird Brothers, Birkenhead. 1873.

20. WHOLE MODEL of H.M.'s armour-plated turret ship "CAPTAIN." Tons 4,472. Horse-power nominal 900. Built 1869 by Laird Bros., Birkenhead. Laid down 1867.

Lent by Messrs. Laird Brothers, Birkenhead. 1876.

Note.—H.M.S. "CAPTAIN," built of iron, on the designs of the late Captain Cowper Coles, R.N. (1866), was lost off the coast of Spain on the night of the 6th September 1870, while keeping station with the Channel Squadron.

The length of the ship was 335 ft., beam 53 ft. 3 ins.; draught of water, 23 ft. 6 ins.; displacement, 7,650 tons.

The vessel was full ship-rigged and carried tripod masts and yards of iron. She had a poop and forecastle, and a spar deck 26 feet wide running her entire length. She was driven by two pair of double engines and twin screws. Engine cylinders 80 ins. diameter, with 3 ft. 3 ins. stroke. The effective power of these engines was 5,400 horse-power. Steam was supplied to them by 8 boilers with 28 furnaces.

H.M.S. "CAPTAIN" carried 6 rifled guns. In each of her turrets (2) were two 25-ton guns, 600-prs.; one 6½-ton 100-pr. gun in her bow; and one 6½-ton 100-pr. gun in her stern, for chasing. Her hull armour plates were 7 and 8 ins. thick, backed with teak 12 ins. thick, fastened to ship's skin 1½ ins. thick. The turret plates were 9 and 10 ins. thick. The upper deck was carried on iron beams 14 ins. deep, covered with iron plating 1½ and 1 in. thick and teak planking 6 ins. thick. The "CAPTAIN" was entirely built, engined, and fitted by Messrs. Laird Brothers, at Birkenhead.

21. WHOLE MODEL of the gunboats "PARANA" and "URUGUAY," 1873. Length 152 ft., breadth 25 ft., depth 12 ft. 6 ins., 455 tons, 80 horse-power.

Lent by Messrs. Laird Brothers, engineers and ship-builders, Birkenhead.   1876.

Note.—Iron screw gunboats of modern type, built for the Government of the Argentine Confederation, armed with two 100-pr. Vavasseur pivot guns. Rigged as barques, and fitted with Bevis' patent feathering screw propeller.

22. WHOLE MODEL of the gunboats "FU-SHÊNG" and "CHIEN-SHÊNG," 1875. Length 87 ft., breadth 26 ft., depth 8 ft. 8 ins., 256 tons, 40 horse-power.

Lent by Messrs. Laird Brothers, engineers and ship-builders, Birkenhead.   1876.

Note.—Iron screw gunboats for coast and river defence, built for the Chinese Government, fitted with twin screws, and armed with one 18-ton Vavasseur gun, 450-pr. These vessels steamed out to China through the Suez Canal.

23. WHOLE MODEL of the gunboats "EL PLATA" and "LOS ANDES," 1875. Length 180 ft., breadth 44 ft., depth 11 ft. 9 ins., 1,588 tons. 750 indicated horse-power.

Lent by Messrs. Laird Brothers, engineers and ship-builders, Birkenhead.   1876.

Note.—Armour-plated twin screw turret vessels, built for the Government of the Argentine Confederation. Protected with armour 6 inches on the hull and 8 inches on the turret, and carrying each two 12½-ton 300-pr. rifled guns. They steam 9½ knots on a load draught of water of 9 ft. 6 ins., and steamed from the Mersey to Buenos Ayres in about 50 days, including all stoppages.

24. WHOLE MODEL of the late H. E. I. Co.'s Iron paddle steamer "NAPIER," 1843. Length 160 ft., breadth 24 ft. Tons 446. Horse-power 90.

Lent by Messrs. Laird Brothers, engineers and shipbuilders, Birkenhead.   1876.

Note.—Built for the Hon. East India Company on a plan patented by Mr. Laird in 1843, with a spoon-shaped bow, and lifting dead wood and rudder.

This form of vessel combines speed, light draught of water, and good steering, with great carrying capacity, and was found to answer so well for the difficult navigation of the river Indus that a large number of river steamers were afterwards constructed by Mr. Laird for the Hon. East India Company on the same system.

25. WHOLE MODEL of the "MARAJO," 1874. Iron paddle steamer. Length 221 ft., breadth 32 ft., depth 10 ft. 3 ins., 1,099 tons, 200 horse power.

Lent by Messrs. Laird, Brothers, Engineers and Shipbuilders, Birkenhead.   1876.

Note.—Type of river steamer of modern construction, having large carrying capacity for passengers and cargo, on a light draught of water, with great speed. Fitted with compound oscillating engines.

26. WHOLE MODEL of the "EARL SPENCER," 1874. Iron paddle steamer. Length 253 ft. 6 ins., breadth 29 ft., depth 14 ft. 9 ins. Tons, 1,067. 350 horse-power.

Lent by Messrs. Laird, Brothers, Engineers and Shipbuilders, Birkenhead.   1876.

Note.—Showing present type of steamers for passenger and cattle traffic. Built for the London and North-western Railway Company for service between Holyhead and Greenore. Speed 15 knots.

See also pages 28-32.

27. WHOLE MODEL of the City of Dublin Steam Packet Company's paddle mail steamer " CONNAUGHT," running between Kingstown and Holyhead. Length 348 ft., width 35 ft., depth 20 ft. 3 in., tonnage 2,039, nominal horse-power 720. Diameter of cylinders 98 inches, length of stroke 6 ft. 6 in. Speed 21 statute miles per hour. Makers of the engines, which are on the oscillating principle, Messrs. Ravenhill, Salkeld, and Co., London. The ship was designed and built by Messrs. John Laird, Sons, and Co., Birkenhead, and launched in 1860.

Lent by Messrs. Laird Brothers, Birkenhead. 1869.

See No. 5, page 66.

28. WHOLE MODEL of the first Iron steamers built on the Thames. The "LORD W. BENTINCK," " MAGNA,"·and " JUMNA," in 1832, for the Honourable East India Company, for the navigation of the river Ganges. Designed and built by Messrs. Maudslay, Sons, and Field.

Presented by Messrs. Maudslay, Sons, and Field. 1866.

29. WHOLE MODEL of the iron screw steamer " MEDWAY," tons 1,464, nominal horse-power 250. Designed and built by Messrs. Oswald and Co.

42594.   B

This steamer was employed, in conjunction with the " GREAT EASTERN " steamship, in laying the Atlantic tele- graph cable, 1866.

Lent by Messrs. Oswald & Co., Sunderland.   1867.

30. MODEL of an Iron Screw Steamer, built and designed by Messrs. Oswald and Co., for the Baltic or Mediterranean trade.

Note.—The principal dimensions of this trading steamer are :—Length over all 206 feet ; breadth, extreme 28 feet 10 inches ; depth 18 feet 4 inches ; tonnage, B.M., 806 ; Register gross 750 ; draft, light 7 feet ; laden 16 feet ; horse-power 100 nominal ; diameter of cylinders 36 inches ; stroke 26 inches.

Lent by Messrs. Oswald & Co., Sunderland.   1867.

. **31.** WHOLE MODEL of the Cunard iron paddle steamer " SCOTIA." Built 1861. Constructed for the British and North American (Cunard) Royal Mail Steam Packet Com- pany by R. Napier & Sons, Glasgow.

Presented by Messrs. R. Napier & Sons, Glasgow.
1867.

Note.—The principal dimensions of the paddle steamship " SCOTIA " are :—Length 366 feet, breadth 47 feet 6 inches, tonnage, builder's measurement, 4,050, load displacement 6,520 tons, horse-power 1,000 nominal. Diameter of cylinders 100 inches, length of stroke 12 feet. The engines are on the principle known as the side lever, and were constructed by Messrs. R. Napier & Sons.

Diameter of paddle wheels 40 feet.

Size of floats, 11 feet 6 inches by 2 feet.

The " SCOTIA " may be said to be the last of the ocean going paddle steamers for commercial purposes, screw propeller vessels having superseded them. It may there- fore be interesting to add, that the first steamer which crossed the Atlantic and traded regularly between England and America was the paddle steamer " GREAT WESTERN," engined by Messrs. Maudslay, Sons, and Field in 1838. She was 1,340 tons burthen, and driven by side lever engines of 420 horse-power, having cylinders 74 inches diameter and 7 feet stroke. Her paddle wheels were 28 feet diameter, and the floats 28 in number were 1 foot 10 inches wide. The wheels made 10 to 18 revolutions per minute. The boilers were 4 in number, with return flues, and the working steam pressure in them was 5 lbs. on the square inch. The " GREAT WESTERN " was built of wood by Patterson of Bristol, and launched in 1837. She was broken up in 1856. Her length was 212 feet ; breadth 35 feet 4 inches ; depth 23 feet 2 inches. Her average speed was 9½ to 10 knots per hour.

32. WHOLE MODEL of the Montreal Ocean Steamship Company's screw steamers "HIBERNIAN" and "NORWEGIAN." Designed and built by W. Denny and Brothers, Dumbarton. Scale ¼ inch to 1 foot. This model shows on the port side the internal arrangements of cabins, engine-room, &c.

> *Note.*—The dimensions of the steamships "HIBERNIAN" and "NORWEGIAN" are:—Length of keel and fore rake 292 feet; breadth, beam, moulded, 37 feet 9 inches; depth moulded, 33 feet; tonnage, o.m. 2,041; horse-power 400, nominal.

> Lent by Messrs. W. Denny and Brothers, Dumbarton, N.B. 1865.

33. WHOLE MODEL of the screw steamer "CITY OF PARIS," belonging to the Liverpool, New York, and Philadelphia Steam Shipping Company (*Inman Line*). Tons 2,740, nominal horse-power 550. Launched December 1865.

> Presented by Mr. William Inman, the Inman Company, Liverpool. 1866.

> *Note.*—The screw steamship "CITY OF PARIS," of the Inman line of Atlantic steamers, was built of iron and fitted out in 1866 by Messrs. Tod and MacGregor of Glasgow, now D. and W. Henderson & Co. Her dimensions are:— Length 365 ft.; beam 40 ft. 4 ins.; depth 26 ft. 2 ins.; tonnage B.M. 2,875. Diameter of her engine cylinders 89 inches. Length of stroke 3 ft. 6 ins. Scale of model ¼-in. to 1 foot. This ship made a remarkable voyage for speed across the Atlantic from New York to Liverpool in (March) 1869, in company with the iron screw steamship "RUSSIA" of the Cunard line. The "RUSSIA" was built in 1867 by Messrs. J. and G. Thomson of Glasgow, and is rather larger than the "CITY OF PARIS," being 3,100 tons B.M. She has engine cylinders 86 ins. in diameter with a stroke 3 ft. 10 ins.

34. WHOLE MODEL of the West India and Pacific Steam Shipping Company's screw steamer "VENEZUELAN." Length 259 feet 5 in., breadth 32 feet 1 in., depth, extreme, 28 feet 9 in. Tons 1,682, horse-power 220. Makers of the engines, Messrs. Jas. Jack and Company, Liverpool. Launched 1865. Built by Messrs. Jones, Quiggin, and Company, Liverpool.

> Lent by the West India and Pacific Steam Shipping Company. 1868.

35. WHOLE MODEL of the West India and Pacific Steam Shipping Company's screw steamer "BOLIVAR."

Length 240 feet, breadth 32 feet 5 in., depth 19 feet 7 in.
Tons 1,250, horse-power 200.   Maker of the engines, J. C.
Thompson, Newcastle-on-Tyne.   Direct acting inverted
cylinder engines ; diameter of cylinders 49 inches.   Stroke
2 feet 6 inches. Launched 1862. Built by Messrs. Richardson, Duck, and Company, Stockton-on-Tees.
    Lent by the West India and Pacific Steam Shipping
    Company.   1868.

36. WHOLE MODEL of the blockade-runner paddle
wheel steamer " EVELYN."   Length 230 ft., breadth of beam
28 ft., draught of water with 1,000 bales of cotton on board
7 ft.   Tons 284 N.M. ; horse-power 200.   Speed at full
power, 17 knots.   Built in 1864 by Messrs. Randolph,
Elder, & Co., Glasgow.
    The late Capt. Hugh Talbot Burgoyne, R.N.   1865.

37. WHOLE MODEL of a proposed Iron-clad Ship of
war, with retreating sides, and fore and aft projections
built in watertight compartments.   The armour plating to
be 3 feet in thickness, and 12 feet in depth.   The upper
white line on the hull of the Model shows the fighting
floatation line of the ship.   The lower white line represents the sea-going line of ship.   The ship is proposed to
be driven by single or twin screw propulsion.   Its system
of construction patented in 1872.   Scale of model ⅛th of
an inch to 1 foot.
    Lent by Dr. J. Collis Browne, 34, Leadenhall Street.
    E.C.   1874.

38. WHOLE MODEL, rigged, of the Imperial German
armour-plated ship of war, " KONIG WILHELM ;" designed
by Mr. E. J. Reed.   Built 1869 by the Thames Iron Works
and Shipbuilding Co.

> *Note.*—The ship's principal dimensions are :— Length
> 355 feet ; breadth 60 feet ; depth 41 feet 9 inches ; tons
> 6,000 ; horse-power, 1,150, nominal.   Engines by Messrs.
> Maudslay, Sons, & Field.

    Lent by E. J. Reed, Esq., M.P., C.B.   1876.

39. WHOLE MODEL of the screw steamship " FARADAY ; "
constructed for Messrs. Siemens Brothers specially for em-
ployment in carrying and laying electric telegraph cables
or ocean telegraph lines.
    Lent by Dr. C. W. Siemens, Queen Anne's Gate,
    Westminster.   1874.

> *Note.*—The " FARADAY " was built, entirely of iron, in
> 1874, by Mitchell and Co., Newcastle.   Her length is 361

feet; breadth 52 feet; depth in hold 36 feet; draught laden 26 feet. Registered tonnage 4,908. Carrying capacity 5,850 tons. She is double-bottomed and flat.
The ship has three cable tanks, each 27 feet deep. Two are of 45 feet diameter, and one is of 37 feet. In these tanks the telegraph cable lies in water and coiled round a hollow cone of iron reaching from the bottom to the top of them. To keep the ship at a uniform draught of water while paying out the cable, these cones carry water from the sea, as well as the tanks and her double bottom; the ship is thus uniformly ballasted. Her engines on the compound system with surface condensers drive twin screws. They are each of 250 horse-power, nominal. The high pressure cylinders are 39 inches diameter, the low pressure 68 inches. The stroke is 48 inches. The engines were built by T. Clark and Co., Newcastle.
Six boilers containing the total heating surface of 9,000 square feet supply steam. The screw propellers are each 16 feet in diameter.

40. WHOLE MODEL iron screw steamship "GLENARTNEY," of the "Glen" line Company's Clipper Screw Steamships for the China trade. These vessels are employed between London and China direct viâ Suez Canal.

Lent by Messrs. MacGregor, Gow, & Co., East India Avenue, E.C. 1874.

Note.—This model represents a fleet of steamers of about the following dimensions:—Length 330 feet; breadth 35 feet; depth 25 feet; tons gross 2,106; horse power 330, nominal.

The model exhibited is a whole model, full rigged, of the screw steamship "GLENARTNEY." Built 1873-74 by the London and Glasgow Iron Shipbuilding and Engineering Company, Glasgow. This vessel in 1874 ran from China (Woosung) to London viâ Suez Canal in 44 days.

The "GLENARTNEY" is fitted with compound inverted cylinder engines of 330 horse-power, nominal.

A still larger and more powerful vessel the "GLENEAGLES" was launched in 1876-77 for the "Glen" line. She maintains a speed of about 14 knots per hour.

The model of the "GLENARTNEY" is on a ¼ scale.

41. WHOLE MODEL of the first screw-steamer in the British Navy, "MERMAID" afterwards named the "DWARF." Built in 1840. Purchased from J. and G. Rennie by the British Admiralty, according to Sir George Cockburn's advice, and on the condition that she should steam 12 miles per hour (7th March 1842). Tried 15th May 1843. Mean speed of 6 runs, 12·142 miles.

Lent by Messrs. J. and G. Rennie, Engineers, Holland Street, Blackfriars. 1876.

42. WHOLE MODEL of twin screw Gun-boats. Built for the Spanish Government by J. and G. Rennie. 1859. Length 90 ft., breadth 14 ft., draught 2 ft. 6 in.; horse-power, 30.

> Lent by Messrs. J. and G. Rennie, Engineers, Holland Street, Blackfriars.   1876.

43. WHOLE MODEL of twin screw Gun-boats. Built for the East Indian Government by J. and G. Rennie, 1857. Length 70 ft., breadth 11 ft., draught 2 ft. 6 in.; nominal horse-power 20, indicated horse-power 76 ; speed 9¼ miles. Armament one long brass 12-pr. gun ; 18 cwt.

> Lent by Messrs. J. and G. Rennie, Engineers, Holland Street, Blackfriars.   1876.

44. WHOLE MODEL of Brazilian twin-screw ironclad gun-boats "COLOMBO" and "CABRAL." Built by J. and G. Rennie, 1866. Length 160 ft., breadth 34 ft. depth 17 ft.; tons, 858 B.M.; nominal horse-power 240 : speed 10 knots. Armament, 4 68 prs.

> Lent by Messrs. J. and G. Rennie, Engineers, Holland Street, Blackfriars.   1876.

45. WHOLE MODEL of H.M. twin screw gun-boats "ARROW" and "BONETTA." Built by J. and G. Rennie, 1871. Length 85 ft., breadth 26 ft., depth 8 ft. 10 in.; tons 244. Armament one 18-ton gun.

> Lent by Messrs. J. and G. Rennie, Engineers, Holland Street, Blackfriars.   1876.

46. WHOLE MODEL of Indian Famine Relief Steamers. Built by J. and G. Rennie, 1874. Date of order, 24th February. Date of launch, 30th March. Tried under steam, 4th April. Length 90 ft., beam 14 ft., depth 5 ft. 6 in.; indicated horse-power 100. Built complete with engines in 35 working days.

> Lent by Messrs. J. and G. Rennie, Engineers, Holland Street, Blackfriars.   1876.

47. WHOLE MODEL of the merchant sailing ship "CYGNET" on launching ways. The port side built, starboard side showing ship's framing and disposition of timbers. Scale ¼ inch to 1 foot.

> Lent by Mr. A. T. Lowe.   1870.

48. WHOLE MODEL of the iron sailing ship "DURHAM." Designed and built by Messrs. Oswald & Co. For Messrs. Temperley, Carter, & Co., London.

Note.—The principal dimensions of the sailing ship "DURHAM" are :—Length over all . 209 feet 6 inches; breadth 34 feet 9 inches; depth 20 feet 9 inches; tonnage B.M., 1,131; register, 998; draft, light 8 feet 2½ inches; laden 18 feet 4½ inches; displacement at load line 1,378 tons.

Lent by Messrs. Oswald & Co., Sunderland.　　1867.

49. WHOLE MODEL of the clipper merchant sailing ship "FIERY CROSS." Built 1861, for the China tea trade, by Chaloner, Hart, and Co., Liverpool. Designed by Mr. Rennie.

A previous ship built, 1855, by Messrs. Rennie and Rankiee, Liverpool, from designs by Mr. Rennie. Dimensions are as follows:—Extreme length 185 feet, extreme breadth 31 ft. 3 in., depth 19 ft. 6 in. Tonnage, o.m. 363, register 702. Displacement 1,615·84 tons. Scale ¼ in. to 1 ft.

Lent by Mr. J. Campbell.　　1869.

See also No. 39, page 32.

50. WHOLE MODEL, rigged complete, of a Dutch galiot of the period 1774–1778. The model bears these dates. It is richly carved throughout, specially at the bow and stern, hatchways, leeboards, &c. Length of model 3 ft. 2 in., beam 12 in.

　-　Purchased from Van Vliet and Co.　　1871.

51. WHOLE MODEL of the merchant sailing vessel "ANTELOPE." Built in the year 1757.

Lent by Mr. James J. Young, West Docks, South Shields.　　1876.

52. WHOLE MODEL of the merchant sailing vessel "BROTHERLY LOVE." Built in the year 1764, and is said to be still reigning, 1876. The mark on the side represents damage from a collision with a steamer some years ago.

Lent by Mr. James Young, West Docks, South Shields.　　1876.

53. WHOLE MODEL in bone of a Three-decker Line-of-battle Ship, made by French prisoners in England during the Peninsular War, 1812.

Lent by Mr. Vaughan Pendred, C.E.　　1876.

CLASS II.

Half Block Models, of Sailing Ships and Steam Ships, showing Lines and Forms.

1. HALF MODEL of the Peninsular and Oriental Company's screw steamer "DELHI." Tons 1,898, horse-power 400. Makers of the engines, Messrs, Ravenhill, Easton, and Company. Launched September 1863. Built by Messrs. Money Wigram and Sons.

> Lent by the Peninsular and Oriental Steam Navigation Company.   1868.

2. HALF MODEL of the Peninsular and Oriental Company's screw steamer "CHARKIEH." Tons 1,615, horse-power 350. Makers of the engines, Messrs. J. and G. Rennie. Launched December 1864. Built by the Thames Iron Works Company, Limited.

> Lent by the Peninsular and Oriental Steam Navigation Company.   1868.

3. HALF MODEL of the Peninsular and Oriental Company's screw steamer "DAKAHLIEH." Tons 1,553, horse-power 350. Makers of the engines, Messrs. J. and G. Rennie. Launched February 1865. Built by Messrs. Money Wigram and Sons.

> Lent by the Peninsular and Oriental Steam Navigation Company.   1868.

4. HALF MODEL of the Peninsular and Oriental Company's screw steamer "TANJORE." Tons 1,971, horse-power 400. Makers of the engines, Messrs. Ravenhill, Easton, and Company. Launched April 1865. Built by the Thames Iron Works Company, Limited.

> Lent by the Peninsular and Oriental Steam Navigation Company.   1868.

5. HALF MODEL of the Peninsular and Oriental Company's screw steamer "SURAT." Tons 2,578, horse-power 500. Makers of the engines, Messrs. C. A. Day and Company. Launched March 1866. Built by Messrs. C. A. Day and Company, Southampton.

> Lent by the Peniusular and Oriental Steam Navigation Company.   1868

6. HALF MODEL of the Peninsular and Oriental Company's screw steamer "GOLCONDA." Tons 1,909. Horse power 400. Launched 2nd December 1863, by the Thames Iron Works Company. Length (register) 314 ft. 3 in., breadth 38 ft. 3 in., depth 26 ft. 6 in. Engines (Wolf's double cylinder) by Messrs. Humphreys & Tennant.

Presented by the Peninsular and Oriental Company. 1865.

7. HALF MODEL of the Peninsular and Oriental Company's paddle steamer "NYANZA." Horse power 450. Engines (oscillating) by Mr. H. G. Rennie. Launched 3rd November 1864, by the Thames Iron Works Company. Length (register) 327 ft. 3 in., breadth 36 ft. 2 in., depth 27 ft. 6 in. Tonnage 2,082.

Presented by the Peninsular and Oriental Company. 1865.

8. SERIES of HALF BLOCK MODELS, presented in 1867 by Messrs. R. Napier & Sons, Glasgow, illustrating the designs for, and interior arrangement of ships of war, on the combined Turret and Broadside system, proposed by the late Admiral E. P. Halsted, R.N. Designed May 1866.

See also Models, No. 5, Class I., page 8.

8a. Half block Model of proposed ship of war "POWERFUL," classed as a second rate. 6 Turrets.

Turrets · - - - 6
Number of guns in turrets - 12
Length of ship 438 ft. 9 in. Breadth 67 ft. 6 in. Depth 28 ft. Load draught 26 ft. 6 in. Tonnage 9,652, builders' old measurement. Displacement, 13,200 tons.

Note.—This model is on a mahogany stand, and fitted to blocks. The starboard side shows the ship as completely constructed. The port side gives a longitudinal through section of the ship's internal arrangement.

Designed May 1866. Scale ¼ inch to 1 foot.

8b. Half block Model of proposed ship · of war "DAUNTLESS," classed as a third rate. 5 Turrets.

Turrets - - - - 5
Number of guns in turrets - 10
Length of ship 422 ft. 6 in. Breadth 65 feet. Depth 28 feet. Load draught 26 feet 6 inches.

Tonnage 8,618, builders' old measurement. Displacement 12,100 tons.

Designed May 1866.   Scale ¼ in. to 1 foot.

Note.—This model hangs at back of case. The starboard side shows the ship completely constructed. The port side gives a longitudinal through section of the ship's internal arrangement.

8c. Half block Model of the proposed ship of war "FORMIDABLE," classed as a fourth rate. 4 Turrets.

Turrets -   -   -   -   4
Number of guns in turrets   -   8
Length of ship 390 ft. Breadth 60 ft. Depth 26 ft. 6 in. Load draught 25 ft. 6 in. Tonnage 6,778, builders' old measurement. Displacement, 10,000 tons.

Designed May 1866.   Scale ¼-inch to 1 foot.

Note.—This model hangs at back of case. The starboard side shows the ship completely constructed. The port side gives a longitudinal through section, showing the ship's internal arrangement.

8d. Half block Model of the proposed ship of war "DEFENCE," classed as a fifth rate. 3 Turrets.

Turrets   -   -   -   -   3
Number of guns in turrets   -   -   6
Length of ship 373 ft. 9 in.   Breadth 57 ft. 6 in. Depth 26 ft. 6 in. Load draught 25 ft. 6 in. Tonnage 5,906, builders' old measurement. Displacement, 9,100 tons.

Designed May 1866.   Scale ¼-inch to 1 foot.

Note.—The model shows starboard side, ship as completely constructed. The port side gives a longitudinal through section, showing the ship's internal arrangement. This model hangs at back of case.

8f. Half block Model of the proposed ship of war "VIGILANT," classed as a seventh rate. 2 Turrets.

Turrets   -   -   -   -   2
• Number of guns in turrets   -   -   4
Length of ship 346 ft. 3 in.   Breadth 52 ft. 6 in. Depth 25 ft. Load draught 24 ft. 6 in. Tonnage 4,615, builders' old measurement. Displacement, 7,400 tons.

Designed May 1866.   Scale ¼ inch to 1 foot.

Note.—This model hangs at back of case. The starboard side shows ship completely constructed. The port side gives a longitudinal through section, showing the ship's internal arrangement.

See also Models, No. 5, p. 8, and No. 3, p. 83.

9. HALF BLOCK MODEL of H.M.'s ship "WATER-WITCH," built of iron, 2 guns, 160 horse-power. Scale ¼-inch to 1 foot. Length 162 ft., breadth 32 ft., draught of water 10 ft. 10 in. forward, 11 ft. 4 in. aft, tonnage 778. Displacement 1,190 tons, speed 9·255 knots. Area of midship section immersed 344 square feet. Built by contract by the Thames Iron Shipbuilding Company, in the River Thames. Laid down in November 1864; launched in June 1866.

Designed by Rear-Admiral Geo. Elliot and the Controller's Department, Admiralty. Propelled on the hydraulic or Turbine principle, invented and patented by Mr. D. Ruthven.

The armament was two 6-ton rifled guns.

The complement of men was 80. 1869.

10. HALF BLOCK MODEL of the screw steamships " MATABAN " and " IRRAWADDY." The British and Burmese Steam Navigation Company. Keel length 340 ft., breadth 36 ft., depth 28 ft. Tons, register, 2,514. Built 1874, by W. Denny and Brothers.

Lent by Messrs. W. Denny and Brothers, Dumbarton. 1874.

11. HALF BLOCK MODEL of screw steamships " VENETIA," " LOMBARDY," " GWALIOR," and " NYZAM." The Peninsular and Oriental Steam Navigation Company. Keel length 350 ft., breadth 38 ft., depth 28 ft. 9 in. Tons 2,513. Built 1873, by W. Denny and Brothers.

Lent by Messrs. W. Denny and Brothers, Dumbarton. 1874.

12. HALF BLOCK MODEL of the screw steamships " CATHAY " and " HYDASPES." African mail ships. Keel length 360 ft., breadth 39 ft., depth 30 ft. 3 in. Tons, o.m. 2,723. Built 1872, by W. Denny and Brothers.

Lent by Messrs. W. Denny and Brothers, Dumbarton. 1874.

13. HALF BLOCK MODEL of the Royal Mail screw steamship " BOYNE." Keel length 358 ft. 6 in., breadth

40 ft. 5 in., depth 34 ft. 6 in. Tons, o.m., 2,882. Built 1871, by W. Denny and Brothers.

> The above four Models lent by Messrs. W. Denny and
> Brothers, Dumbarton.   1874.

14. HALF BLOCK MODEL of the Atlantic screw steamers "NEVADA" and "IDAHO." Liverpool and New York line. Built 1868, for the Liverpool and Great Western Steamship Company, by the Palmer's Shipbuilding Company, Limited. Length 352 ft. ; breadth 43 ft. ; depth 30 ft. Tonnage gross 3,132 ; horse-power 440 nominal ; speed 13 knots per hour. Scale $\frac{1}{36}$ full size.

> Lent by the Palmer's Shipbuilding Company, Limited,
> Newcastle-on-Tyne.   1874.

15. HALF-BLOCK MODEL of the steam screw yacht "CORNELIA," built 1868, for Earl Vane, by the Palmer's Shipbuilding Company, Limited. Length 176 ft. ; breadth 20¾ ft. ; depth 14 ft. Tonnage gross 212 ; horse-power 50 nominal ; speed 11 knots per hour. Scale $\frac{1}{48}$th full size.

> Lent by the Palmer's Shipbuilding Company Limited,
> Newcastle-on-Tyne.   1874.
> See also Nos. 16, 17, and 18, pages 11, 12.

16. HALF MODEL showing the External iron riders of H.M.S. "CALEDONIA," iron-cased frigate, built in 1863 at Woolwich.

> Lent by Mr. George Turner, late Master Shipwright,
> Woolwich Dockyard.   1864.

17. HALF MODEL of Messrs. Westwood and Baillie's design for an armour-plated Turret ship, showing broadside, and fore and aft angular firing. Tons 6,300. Guns 22. Horse-power 1,160 nominal.

> Lent by Messrs. Westwood and Baillie.   1867.

18. HALF MODEL of Messrs. Jardine, Mathison, and Co's. paddle steamer "GLENGYLE," constructed for the navigation of the river Yangtzee. Tons 2,040, nominal horse-power 400. Designed and built by W. Denny and Brothers, Dumbarton.

> Presented by Messrs. W. Denny and Brothers, Dum-
> barton, N.B.   1865.

19. HALF MODEL of a Corvette of the "ALABAMA" class.

> Proposed by Mr. George Turner, late Master Ship-
> wright, Woolwich Dockyard.
> Lent.   1864.

Note.—During the civil war in America, 1860–1864, the American Confederate States celebrated corvette "ALABAMA," built in England, was sunk in an action fought off Cherbourg on 19th June 1864, with the Federal ship-of-war "KERSAGE."

20. HALF BLOCK MODEL of the circular armour-plated Russian ships of war "POPOVKA," "ADMIRAL POPOFF."
Lent by the Russian Embassy.   1876.

Note.—There are two of these circular iron-clad ships of war constructed by Russia herself for the Imperial Navy, respectively the "NOVGOROD," and "ADMIRAL POPOFF." The principal dimensions of the latter are, extreme diameter 121 feet, mean draught of water 13 feet, height of upper deck at side from load water-line amidships 1 ft. 6 in., height of barbette turret from load water-line 13 ft. 3 in., displacement 3,553 tons. This vessel carries two 41-ton guns, which can be trained completely round inside the turret. The gun carriages are arranged to allow the guns to be lowered down behind the turret for loading and aiming, and to be brought up for firing. Besides the heavy guns, there are on each side of the superstructure, which contains cabins and quarters for the crew, two smaller guns of sufficient power to penetrate an unarmoured enemy. The armour plating of the vessel and turret is in two solid layers, having a total thickness of 1 foot 6 in. (including equivalent thickness for the hollow iron girders behind the armour). The side armour of the vessel extends from the edge of the upper deck down to 4 ft. 6 in. below load water-line. The upper deck is protected by deck armour 3 inches thick, which extends from the circumference of the turret to the circumference of the vessel. The ship is propelled by eight compound vertical engines each of 80 nominal horse-power. Four of these engines each work an independent screw of 10 ft. 6 in. diameter. The other four engines, arranged and worked in pairs, drive the middle screws of the ship which are larger than the others and lower down, deeper in the water. The speed of the "ADMIRAL POPOFF" is estimated at 9 to 10 knots per hour. She is launched, but not yet completed for sea. The vessel is built of iron, with a double bottom, and is sheathed with wood and copper. The principal objects of the design of this circular ironclad are :—

1. Heavy armour and gun-carrying power, upon a limited draught of water.
2. Great steadiness of gun platform, ensuring efficient working of the guns at sea.
3. Complete protection of hull and battery by uniform thickness of armour throughout.
4. Cheapness of construction.
5. Numbers of compartments around the central vital parts of the ship which are specially effective for saving the vessel in case of torpedo attack.

21. MODEL of the "JOHN RANDOLPH," 1834. Paddle steamer. Length 110 ft., breadth 22 ft., depth 7 ft. 6 ins. 249 tons. 60 horse-power.

Lent by Messrs. Laird Brothers, Engineers and Ship-builders, Birkenhead.   1876.

Note.—The first iron steamer ever seen on American waters. Built at Birkenhead, taken to pieces, shipped at Liverpool, rivetted together on the Savannah river, where for many years after she did service as a tug boat.

22. HALF BLOCK MODEL of the "GARRYOWEN," 1834. Paddle steamer.   Length 130 ft., breadth 21 ft. 6 ins., depth 9 ft. 3 inches.   263 tons.   90 horse-power.

Lent by Messrs. Laird Brothers, Engineers and Ship-builders, Birkenhead.   1876.

Note.—Paddle steamer built for the City of Dublin Steam Packet Company, for the navigation of the lower Shannon, and the largest iron vessel built at this time. After 30 years' service in Ireland the machinery was taken out of her and she was made into a sailing ship.

About the year 1851, at Mr. Laird's suggestion, this vessel was placed at the disposal of the Admiralty to enable them to institute a series of experiments on the variation of the compass in iron vessels, which were conducted by Capt. Johnson, R.N., and subsequently elaborated by the experiments carried out by Professor Airy on the General Steam Navigation Company's steamer "RAINBOW" built by Mr. Laird in 1837.

23. HALF BLOCK MODEL, of H.E.I.C. Paddle steamers "EUPHRATES" and "TIGRIS," 1834.   Length 105 ft., breadth 19 ft., depth 7 ft. 6 ins. Tons, 179. 50 horse-power.

Lent by Messrs. Laird Brothers, Engineers and Ship-builders, Birkenhead.   1876.

Note.—Built for the Hon. East India Company for General Chesney's expedition for the exploration of the River Euphrates. These vessels were built by Mr. Laird at Birkenhead, 1834, then taken to pieces and shipped to the coast of Syria, and after having been carried across the desert by camels, they were put together and launched on the banks of the Euphrates by artisans sent from Birkenhead for the purpose.

Three similar vessels of very light draught, the "NIMROD," "NITOCRIS," and "ASSYRIA," of 153 tons, each carrying two 9-pr. pivot guns, were built for the navigation of the Tigris and Euphrates a few years later.

24. BLOCK MODEL of a frigate prepared by the late William Laird, in 1836, to show application of the screw propeller to ships of war or vessels of large size.

Lent by Messrs. Laird Brothers, Engineers and Ship-builders, Birkenhead.   1876.

25. HALF BLOCK MODEL of the "ROBERT F. STOCKTON," 1838. Iron screw steamer. Length 63 ft. 5 ins., breadth 10 ft., depth 7 ft. 33 tons. 30 horse-power.

Lent by Messrs. Laird Brothers, Engineers and Ship-builders, Birkenhead. 1876.

Note.—One of the first screw steamers ever built; fitted with Ericsson's screw propeller.

The propeller was unshipped for the voyage made under canvass from Liverpool to New York, where she was employed for many years as a tug boat.

26. HALF BLOCK MODEL of H.E.I.C. paddle steamer "NEMESIS," 1839. Length 169 ft., breadth 29 ft., depth 10 ft. 3 ins. 660 tons. 120 horse-power.

Lent by Messrs. Laird Brothers, Engineers and Ship-builders, Birkenhead. 1876.

Note.—The paddle steamer "NEMESIS" was built of iron for the Hon. East India Company for service on the coast of India, and armed with two 32-pr. pivot guns.

This vessel, as well as the "PHLEGETHON," a similar but rather smaller vessel, though only drawing 5 feet of water, made the passage out to India round the Cape, a drop rudder and sliding keel, as shown on model, being fitted for that purpose.

Under the command of Captain (now Admiral) Sir William Hall, R.N., the "NEMESIS" did distinguished service in the China wars, her light draught enabling her to perform service which no wooden vessel in the fleet was able to accomplish.

At the same time the "MEDUSA" and "ARIADNE," of 432 tons, and each carrying two 24-pr. pivot guns, were built for the same service.

27. HALF BLOCK MODEL of the paddle steamer "GUADÁLOUPE," 1842. Length 187 ft., breadth 30 ft., depth 16 ft. 788 tons. 180 horse-power.

Lent by Messrs. Laird Brothers, Engineers and Ship-builders, Birkenhead. 1876.

Note.—The success of the above steamers "NEMESIS," "MEDUSA," and "ARIADNE" (the first iron vessels armed with heavy guns) induced the agents of the Mexican Government to order the steam frigate "GUADALOUPE," of 800 tons and 180 horse-power, armed with two 68-pounder pivot guns, one at each end, and four 24-pounder broadside guns. The satisfactory reports made upon the construction and trials of this vessel by the late Mr. Large and other officers, induced the English Government to entrust Mr. Laird with the designing and building of the iron paddle-wheel frigate "BIRKENHEAD," 1,400 tons, one of the first iron war ships in the English navy ; this ship was launched in 1845.

28. HALF BLOCK MODEL of mail Steamboat "DOVER," 1840. Paddle wheel. Length 113ft., breadth 21 ft., depth 9 ft. 10½ ins. 228 tons. 90 horse-power.

Lent by Messrs. Laird Brothers, Engineers and Ship-builders, Birkenhead. 1876.

Note.—This was the first iron mail steamer, and was built for the Admiralty in 1840. She carried the mails between Dover and Calais for many years, and afterwards did good service on the coast of Africa.

29. HALF BLOCK MODEL of the "HELEN McGREGOR," 1843. paddle steamer. Length 180 ft., breadth 26 ft., depth 15 ft. 573 tons. 220 horse-power.

Lent by Messrs. Laird Brothers, Engineers, and Shipbuilders, Birkenhead. 1876.

Note.—Built for carrying passengers and cattle between Hull and Antwerp ; one of the largest vessels of her class.

30. HALF BLOCK MODEL of mail-boat ; " LORD WARDEN," 1847. Paddle wheel. Length 160 ft., breadth 24 ft., depth 10 ft. 9 ins., 446 tons, 160 horse-power nominal.

Lent by Messrs. Laird Brothers, Engineers, and Shipbuilders, Birkenhead. 1876.

Note.—Built for the South-Eastern Railway Company in 1847, and is still running as one of their despatch boats between Folkstone and Boulogne.

31. HALF BLOCK MODEL of mail-boat "CAMBRIA" 1848. Paddle wheel. Length 196 ft., breadth 27 ft., depth 14 ft. 6 ins. 716 tons. 370 horse-power.

Lent by Messrs. Laird Brothers, Engineers and Shipbuilders, Birkenhead. 1876.

Note.—Built for the Chester and Holyhead Railway Company for their despatch service between Holyhead and Dublin was lengthened in 1860, and is still running as a cattle boat.

32. HALF BLOCK MODEL of the " FORERUNNER " 1852. Iron screw steamer. Length 161 ft. 6 ins., breadth 22 ft., depth 11 ft. 4½ ins. 381 tons. 50 horse-power.

Lent by Messrs. Laird Brothers, Engineers and Shipbuilders, Birkenhead. 1876.

Note.—Built for McGregor Laird, Esq., the founder of the African Royal Mail Steam Navigation Company, of which she was the pioneer vessel.

33. HALF BLOCK MODEL of the "COUNTESS OF ELLES-MERE," 1852. Paddle Steamer. Length 160 ft., breadth 20 ft., depth 7 ft. 6 ins. 315 tons. 80 horse-power.

Lent by Messrs. Laird Brothers, Engineers and Shipbuilders, Birkenhead. · 1876.

Note.—Fast paddle passenger steamer, formerly running on the Mersey, afterwards sold as a yacht to the Grand Duke Constantine of Russia.

34. HALF BLOCK MODEL of the "NUBIA" 1854. Iron screw steamer. Length 292 ft., breadth 39 ft., depth 27 ft. 9 ins. 2,173 tons. 450 horse-power.

Lent by Messrs. Laird Brothers, Engineers and Shipbuilders, Birkenhead. 1876.

Note.—Type of screw mail and passenger steamer of her date. Built for the Peninsular and Oriental Steam Navigation Company, and still carrying the mails in their service.

35. HALF BLOCK MODEL of the mail boats "ULSTER," "MUNSTER," and "CONNAUGHT," 1860. Paddle wheel. Length 334 ft., breadth 35 ft., depth 19 ft. 2,039 tons. 750 horse-power.

Lent by Messrs. Laird Brothers, Engineers and Shipbuilders, Birkenhead. 1876.

Note.—Built for the City of Dublin Steam Packet Company, for the mail service between Holyhead and Kingston, in 1860.

The "CONNAUGHT" attained a speed of over 18 knots, or 21 statute miles per hour on her official trial at Stokes Bay.

These three vessels, together with the "LEINSTER," built by Messrs. Samuda, still perform this service.

36. HALF BLOCK MODEL of the "AFRICA," 1871 : Iron screw steamer. Length 285 ft., breadth 34 ft., depth 23 ft. 3½ ins. 1,627 tons. 200 horse-power.

Lent by Messrs. Laird Brothers, Engineers and Shipbuilders, Birkenhead. 1876.

Note.—One of the modern steamers of the African Royal Mail Company, for same service as " FORERUNNER," built 1852. See No. 32.

37. HALF BLOCK MODELS of the "CORCOVADO," "PUNA," and "BRITANNIA," 1872. Iron screw steamer. Length 375 ft., breadth 43 ft., depth 33 ft. 9 ins. 3,434 tons. 600 horse-power.

Lent by Messrs. Laird Brothers, Engineers and Shipbuilders, Birkenhead. 1876.

Note.—Type of screw mail and passenger steamer of present date.

Built for the mail and passenger service of the Pacific Steam Navigation Company.

The "CORCOVADO" made her first voyage from Liverpool to Callao, 11,000 knots, in 33½ days, equal to a mean speed of 13·54 knots.

See also pages 13–15.

42594.　　　　　　　　　　　　　　　　　　　C

38. HALF BLOCK MODEL of the light-draught iron paddle steamer, "ALOUNGPYAH." Built, 1875. Tons, 825, B.M. Horse-power 150, nominal.

> Lent by R. Duncan & Co., Port Glasgow.   1876.

> *Note.*—The half model of this paddle steamer illustrates the method of carrying a spar deck which has a roof, covering all. Also the detail of upper deck fittings. Her length is 245 feet; breadth 26 feet; depth 8 feet. She carries light goods and passengers, and tows two iron barges each 190 feet long, carrying 300 to 500 tons weight of cargo, according to the season of the year. The engines are compound diagonal, with cylinders 31 and 54 inches diameter. Stroke 54 inches. Two horizontal cylindrical tubular boilers supply steam at 70 lbs. per square inch. The coal bunkers carry 100 tons of coal sufficient for a voyage from Rangoon to Mandalay and back, 1,400 miles. She was built by R. Duncan & Co. for the navigation of the river Irrawaddy, from Rangoon in British Burmah, to Bhamo in Upper Burmah, nearly 1,000 miles.

39. HALF BLOCK MODEL of clipper sailing ship "FIERY CROSS," built 1855. Length 173 ft.; breadth 31 ft. 6 in.; depth 18 ft. 9 in. Tonnage, o.m., 810. Scale ¼ inch to 1 foot.

> Lent by Mr. J. Campbell.   1869.

> *Note.*—This Model represents the ship "FIERY CROSS," built at Liverpool in 1855, by Messrs. Rennie and Rankiee, referred to on page 20, No. 49.

40. HALF BLOCK MODEL of a British merchant clipper sailing ship. Length 170 ft.; beam 28 ft. Scale ¼-inch to 1 foot.

> Lent by Mr. J. Campbell.   1869.

41. HALF MODEL of the iron sailing ship, "VICTORY." Tons 1,198. Built 1863. Designed and built by Messrs. Laurence Hill and Co. for Messrs. Potter, Wilson, and Co., Glasgow.

> Presented by Messrs. Laurence Hill and Co., Glasgow. 1865.

> *Note.*—The "VICTORY" on her first voyage in 1863 ran from the Clyde to Port Chalmers, New Zealand, in 72 days. From anchorage to anchorage 77 days. W. Gibbon, Master.

42. HALF BLOCK MODEL of the ships "JAMES NICHOL FLEMING," and "OTAGO." Built on the composite principle in 1869.

> Lent by R. Duncan & Co., Port Glasgow.   1876.

Note.—The model shows the upper deck plan of the ships, their diagonal iron bracing, and other detail of construction.

Their dimensions are :—
  Length 205 feet.
  Beam 34 feet 6 inches.
  Depth 20 feet 6 inches.
  Tonnage 1,000 gross.

43. HALF BLOCK MODEL of the sailing ship "JAPANESE."
Lent by Mr. W. Roydon, Liverpool.   1876.

44. MODEL of the solid of LEAST RESISTANCE, by the late Andrew John Robertson, dated 1861.
Lent by Mr. Michael Scott, F.R.S.E., London.
                                          1876.

45. HALF BLOCK MODEL of the screw steam-ship "SIR JOHN LAWRENCE." Embodying to a considerable extent the form of least resistance, designed by Michael Scott, in conjunction with the late Andrew John Robertson. The performance of this ship was excellent.
Lent by Mr. Michael Scott, F.R.S.E., London.
                                          1876.

46. HALF BLOCK MODELS representing lines and forms of light-draught vessels for river navigation in British Columbia, 1860.
  Presented   1876.

Note.— These models represent vessels in British Columbia, about 1860.
  The "CARIBO," side wheel steamer. Built at Victoria for the Fraser River trade.
  The river steamer "GOVERNOR DOUGLASS." Built at Victoria. Tons 200. Draught 3 feet.
  Centre-board schooner. Built at Victoria for the British Columbia coasting trade.

C 2

CLASS III.

Models of Construction, Sailing Ships and Steam Ships, Wood and Iron.   Keels, Timbers, Frames, Beams, Knees, &c.   Sectional Models.

1. MODELS, 5 in number, of Ship Construction. Wood and iron. Purchased 1874.

1. Half midship section of a corvette, on ½-in. scale showing the method of ship's framing, fastening beams to ships' sides, &c. Wood construction.

2. Half midship section of an armour-plated ship of war, on ½-in. scale, showing method of the construction of ship's frame, the armour plating and backing, &c. Iron construction.

3. Model showing the present system of framing armour-plated ships of war in Her Majesty's service, with ship's skin plating attached. Scale 1 in. to 1 ft.

4. Half block model, on a scale of ¼ in. to 1 ft., showing the principal lines used in "laying off" the "fore" body of a merchant ship.

5. Half block model, on a scale of ¼ in. to 1 ft., showing the principal lines used in "laying off" the "after" body of a merchant ship.

6. Diagram, showing the lines used in "laying off" the "after" body of a screw frigate. Wood construction.

The foregoing five models and diagram, purchased 1874.

Note.—The above models and diagram, illustrating ship construction, are used for reference in the instruction of students in naval architecture. They are prepared under the direction of the Science and Art Department. Similar models form part of the travelling apparatus for instruction in science, lent by the Department to science schools and classes of this country. A few further explanatory remarks as to what the models are intended to represent may be of service.

1. The model of the half-midship section of the wood ship shows the system now in general use in Her Majesty's dockyards of framing with long and short armed floors in alternation with the ordinary

floors and first futtocks, formerly called cross-pieces and half-floors. The object of this arrangement is to assist the conversion of the timbers, and to improve the shift of butts; the frames having the long and short armed floors are termed filling frames in contradistinction to the regular frames.

2. The model of the half-midship section of the iron-clad ship shows the longitudinal system of framing, as adopted in Her Majesty's ships "AGINCOURT" "MINOTAUR," and "NORTHUMBERLAND," and also the method of forming and combining the several parts of the hull.

3. The small sectional model represents the mode now adopted, in Her Majesty's service of framing iron-clad ships, more particularly of forming and fitting the frame plates, being a modification of that shown by the larger model. The object of this plan is to economise weight of materials and cost of workmanship, and is termed the bracket system of framing.

4–5. The block models are also intended to aid the students in understanding the principles of the geometry of shipbuilding or "laying off;" they show the forms that the several lines assume by the ship, and how she is cut by the different planes.

6. The diagram, as will be seen, represents the after-body of a wood screw ship as laid off. It has not been considered necessary to prepare a similar diagram of the fore-body, as the character of the lines used in "fairing" is nearly identical. *See* Fore-body in Fincham's Laying off.

⁎ These models belong to the Circulating Collection of the Museum which is lent from time to time to country schools of art and science for study. They may not therefore be found at all times in the collection of ship models.

2. MODEL of the section of a ship's side.
Lent by Mr. J. Walker. 1867.

3. MODEL of the section of a ship's side, with armour plates attached.
Lent by Mr. J. Walker. 1867.

4. MODEL of part of the frame of a ship of war, as proposed by Mr. Joseph Tucker.

> Presented by Mr. J. S. Tucker.   1865.

5. Comparative MODEL, showing the oval stern, with quarter ports for guns on each deck.

> Presented by Mr. J. S. Tucker.   1865.

6. Two MODELS of midship sections of vessels.

> Presented by Mr. J. S. Tucker.   1865.

7. MODEL showing a method of total under-side fastenings for deck planking.

> Presented by Mr. J. S. Tucker.   1865.

8. MODEL of the midship section of a design for a four-decked ship of war, the "DUKE OF KENT," to carry 170 guns.

> Proposed by Mr. Joseph Tucker in 1809, when Master Shipwright of Plymouth Dockyard.
> Presented by Mr. J. S. Tucker.   1865.
> See Drawing, No. 40, page 126.

9. Two SPECIMENS of patent grooves and metal sheathing for iron ships.

> Presented by Mr. T. B. Daft, C.E.   1864.

10. SPECIMEN of zinc sheathing for iron vessels ("Daft's" patent). Patented September 1863.

> Presented by Mr. T. B. Daft, C.E.   1865.

11. Two MODELS illustrating plan of wood sheathing for iron ships. Model (marked H.N. 2) shows finish to wood sheathing.

> Proposed by Messrs. Hooper and Nickson, Liverpool.
> Lent by Hooper and Nickson, Liverpool.   1870.

12. THREE MODELS (18 × 12 inches) of the after parts of the submerged propeller ships "ARCHIMEDES," built in 1839, and "NOVELTY," built 1839–40.

> Lent by Mr. Henry Wimshurst, the constructor of the original vessels.   1873.

> 1. Model of the after body of the original experimental vessel, "ARCHIMEDES," built 1839, as prepared for the application of the submerged screw propeller by Mr. H. Wimshurst, Limehouse.

> The model has also attached to it, a model in wood of the original screw propeller applied to the ship and used on her first voyage in May 1839.

2. Model showing the complete framing and construction of the after body of the second submerged propeller or screw steamship, the "NOVELTY" built by Mr. H. Wimshurst, 1839–40.

This vessel was the first to be fitted with direct-acting engines to drive screw propeller, and having means for shipping or unshipping same.

3. Model of the after body of the "NOVELTY," the second screw steamer, built in 1839-40, showing Mr. H. Wimshurst's altered position for the submerged screw propeller.

The above models lent by Mr. H. Wimshurst. 1873.
See Drawings No.69, page 132, and No. 38, page 72.

13. THREE WHOLE MODELS, illustrating the " double-ended principle " in shipbuilding; and one sectional MODEL of an "after end," fitted with nautilus propellers, patented by the late Mr. Kennedy, 28th October 1863.

The largest of these models, which was the first made, dates back to March 1862, and was placed in the Museum of Patents in September 1862. The last one placed there was made for the drawings prepared for the patent. The novel points consist in the new form of bottom, propellers, rudders, battery, &c. The propellers are also the subject of a patent, dated May 1862.

Presented by the late Mr. John Kennedy, White-haven.   1864.

14. MODEL, midship Section, showing the construction of the combined Turret and Broadside Armour-plated iron ships, proposed by the late Vice-Admiral E. P. Halstead, R.N., in 1866.

Scale ½ in. to 1 ft.

Presented by Messrs. R. Napier & Sons, Glasgow.
                1867.

Note.—The system of diagonal trussing for the spar deck is a patent by R. Napier, Esq.

See also No. 5, page 8, No. 18, page 42, No. 3, page 83.

15. Series of WHOLE and HALF BLOCK MODELS, in Wood. 59 in number. Illustrating theoretical principles of ships' lines.

Lent by Mr. John Scott Russell, F.R.S.   1868.

Note.—These models, on about ¼-in. to 1-foot scale, illustrate the gradual development of Mr. John Scott Russell's wave-line system for ship construction, and exhibit intermediate steps from the square box model

(No. 59) to the complete theoretical rendering of the idea in model No. 1. The different models represent the experimental forms used for instruction and comparison. The following MODELS, Nos. 3, 5, 8, 12, 13, 14, 17, 18, 20, 21, 22, 24, 34, 35, 36, represent some of the most successful steamers and yachts which have been built upon the wave-line system by Mr. Russell :—

15—3. Whole Model, complete, on about ¼-in. to 1-foot scale, of the iron paddle-wheel steamship "BARON OSY." Tons, 400. Designed and built 1840, by Mr. J. Scott Russell, and running between London and Antwerp as a passenger and cargo vessel, 1874.

Note.—This "BARON OSY," length about 200 ft., breadth about 26 ft., after 35 years' service as a trader between London and Antwerp was replaced by a new "BARON OSY," built of iron, by Mitchell and Co., Sunderland, 1875, 245 ft. long, 1,100 tons burthen. She has feathering paddle-wheels, and compound engines by Thompson and Co. 300 horse-power, nominal.

15—5. Whole Model, complete, of a small trading screw steamer.

15—8. Whole Model, complete, of the Sydney and Melbourne Royal Mail Steam Packet Company's paddle-wheel steamer "PACIFIC." Tons, 1,470. Horse-power, 500. Designed and built by Mr. J. Scott Russell. See Drawing of Engines, No. 49, page 127.

15—12. Whole Model, complete, of a steam screw collier with long hull.

15—13. Whole Model, complete, of a trading screw steamer.

15—14. Whole Model, complete, of an iron paddle-wheel trading steamer of the "HALDER" class. Built some 25 years ago.

15—17. Whole Model, complete, of a steam screw collier lengthened. A similar vessel to the "EAGLE" and "CAROLINE" iron screw colliers. Built some 25 years ago.

15—18. Whole Model, complete, of a long screw steam collier.

15—20. Whole Model, complete, of the Prussian man-of-war paddle-wheel steamer "DANTZIG," 12 guns, 400 horse-power. Designed and built by Mr. Scott Russell.

15—21. Whole Model, complete, of the paddle-wheel

passenger and trading steamer " ROUEN," running
between Newhaven and Dieppe. Owned by
London, Brighton, and South Coast Railway
Company. See Model No. 11.

15—22. Whole Model, complete, of a passenger and
trading screw steamer, designed and built by
Mr. Scott Russell. The engines and boilers are
placed aft. The passenger saloon and cabin
accommodation is amidships. Further cabin room,
right aft.

15—24. Whole Model, complete, of the iron paddle-
wheel steam yacht "WAVE QUEEN." Designed
and built some 25 years ago by Mr. J. Scott
Russell. This vessel was remarkable for her
extreme length, very narrow breadth, and shallow
depth, all clearly illustrated by this model. She
attained a high rate of speed. Scale of model
¼-in. to 1 foot, representing the vessel's length to
have been about 220 feet, and her beam about
15 feet.

See also Model No. 9.

Models of Theoretical Principles, J. Scott Russell.

15—1. Model, whole block, illustrating solid of least
resistance, with elliptical midship section.

15—2. Whole Model, ribband model, deck retreating.
Starboard side built complete. Port side showing
ribband.

15—4. Theoretical Principles. Block Model, whole,
illustrating lines of ships, buttocks, and water-lines.

15—6. Whole Model of a sailing ship. Starboard
side planked and complete. Port side shows
timbers and waling. Bow portion, the ribband.
Wooden ship construction.

15—7. Whole Model, ribband model. Deck retreating. Wooden ship construction. Port side
shows long ribband. Starboard side unfinished.

15—9. Practical Shipbuilding, block model of the
buttock and water-line of the paddle-wheel steam
yacht "WAVE QUEEN." See Model No. 24.

15—10. Whole Model, ribband model. Wooden ship
construction. Starboard side completely finished.
Port side, ribband.

15--11. Practical Shipbuilding, block model of the
buttock and water-lines of the paddle-wheel
steamer " ROUEN." See Model No. 21.

15—12. Theoretical Principles. Block Model of ship's lines, buttocks, &c.

15—15. Block Model. Whole model, showing lines and buttock of a small steam screw yacht.

15—16. Theoretical Principles. Block Model, whole. Water-line and buttocks.

15—19. Whole Model of the sailing schooner yacht "AMERICA." Built at New York in 1851. Designed by Mr. Steers, N. Y.

15—23. Hollow block Model, showing form and water-line of a lengthened steam screw collier.

15—25. Block Model of the hull and lines of the Prussian gunboats, paddle-wheel steamers, "NIX" and "SALAMANDER," water-line, &c. See Drawing, No. 51, page 127.

15—26. Block Model, whole, showing water-line and form of paddle-wheel steamers built on the lines and model of the "SCHAFFHAUSEN" steamer.

15—27. Half block Model. Key model for a yacht or small vessel.

15—28. Half block Model. Key model for a yacht or small vessel.

15—29. Half block Model. Key model for a yacht or small vessel.

15—30. Block Model, whole, illustrating lines of ships, buttocks, &c.

15—31. Block Model, whole, illustrating lines of ships, buttocks, &c.

15—32. Block Model, whole, of a flat-bottomed shallow boat, for Indian river navigation. Iron construction.

15—33. Half block Model. Buttock lines.

15—34. Whole Model, block, of the sailing yacht "UNDINE." Owned by his Grace the Duke of Sutherland.

15—35. Whole Model, block, of the sailing yacht "THEMIS."

15—36. Whole Model, block, of the schooner sailing yacht "TITANIA."

15—37. Whole Model of a sailing cutter yacht. Form and water-line.

15—38. Theoretical Principles. Block Model. Water-lines of a ship.

15—39. Half block Models. The working model used for the construction of iron ships, giving the sizes and thicknesses of the plates, and other working detail.

15—40. Half block Models. The working model used in the construction of iron ships, giving the sizes and thicknesses of the plates, and other working detail.

15—41. Block Model, whole, of a shallow-draught river steamer, for Indian river navigation. Iron construction.

15—42. Sectional Model, H.M.S. " WARRIOR," built 1860, as originally designed by Mr. Scott Russell, showing proposed method of armour plating, &c.

15—43. Theoretical Principles. Hollow block Model of a ship's hull, showing form and water-line.

15—44. Theoretical Principles. Hollow block Model of a ship's hull, showing form for least resistance, water-line, &c.

15—45. Theoretical Principles. Hollow block Model of a ship's hull, showing form and water-line.

15—46. Theoretical Principles. Hollow block Model of a steamer's hull, showing form and water-line.

15—47. Theoretical Principles. Hollow block Model of a ship's hull, old form, showing form and water-line.

15—48. Hollow block Model of the hull and water-line of the Royal Mail screw steamer " VICTORIA AND ADELAIDE," Australian liner. Designed by Mr. J. Scott Russell.

15—49. Theoretical Principles. Hollow block Model of a long ship's hull, showing form and water-line

15—50. Theoretical Principles. Hollow block Model of the hull of a paddle-wheel steamship with retreating sides for the wheel space.

15—51. Theoretical Principles. Hollow block Model of a steamship's hull. Lines and form on the wave-line principle.

15—52. Theoretical **Principles.** Hollow block Model of a ship's hull, old form.

15—53. Theoretical Principles. Hollow block Model of a ship's hull on the lines of a Dutch galiot.

15—54. Theoretical Principles. Hollow block Model of a long ship's hull, showing form and water-line.

15—55. Theoretical Principles. Hollow block Model, illustrating " wave-line " square sections of a ship's hull.

15—56. Theoretical Principles. Hollow block Model of a ship's hull, old form.

15—57. Whole block Model, showing form and water-line of a ship of war, designed by Mr. Scott Russell.

15—58. Whole block Model, showing form and water-line of a proposed ship of war, designed by Mr. Scott Russell.

15—59. Theoretical Principles. Hollow block Model. Square block form of a hull and water-line.

The foregoing 59 models, illustrating theoretical and practical principles of ship construction, lent by Mr. J. Scott Russell, F.R.S.   1868.
See also Engravings, No. 65, page 129.

16. HALF MODEL, showing a proposal for double bulkheads in iron ships capable of holding water in case of fire ; for strength and security to ship and cargo ; and affording a simple means of testing the tightness of the bulkhead itself. Proposed by Dr. John Taylor, M.D., late Professor of Natural Philosophy in the Andersonian University, Glasgow.
Presented by the late Dr. John Taylor, M.D.   1873.

17. MODEL illustrating McCool's designs and methods for stopping holes in ships' bottoms by means of galvanized iron plates and screw bars.
，· Lent by Mr. J. McCool.   1872.

18. MODEL, designed to illustrate the fore turret and fore deck arrangement, in the proposed combined turret and broadside ships of war, designed by the late Vice-Admiral E. P. Halsted, R.N., in 1866.
Note.—This model shows proposed method for carrying spar deck, and clearing fore part of ship of

hamper, so as to obtain a thorough end on line of fire.

Presented by Messrs. R. Napier & Sons, Glasgow. 1867.

See also No. 14, page 37.

19. MODEL of two half sterns of a first-rate ship of war, wood construction, showing "Blake's" method for the framing of the timber, &c., and gallery. Designed by Mr. R. Blake, Master Shipwright in H.M.'s Dockyards, 1806–1855.

Presented by the Rev. J. Hardie, Falmouth. 1866.

20. MODEL of "Blake's" plan for the prevention of water entering a ship, in the event of any accident to the screw. Designed by Mr. R. Blake, Master Shipwright in H.M.'s Dockyards, 1806–1855.

Presented by the Rev. J. Hardie, Falmouth. 1866.

21. MODEL of "Blake's" plan for connecting beams to ship's side. Designed by Mr. R. Blake, Master Shipwright in H.M.'s Dockyards, 1806–1855.

Presented by the Rev. J. Hardie, Falmouth. 1866.

22. MODEL on "Blake's" plan of futtock timbers, fitted with side chock. Designed by Mr. R. Blake, Master Shipwright in H.M.'s Dockyards, 1806–1855.

Presented by the Rev. J. Hardie, Falmouth. 1866.

23. MODEL on "Blake's" plan of futtock timber with side scarf. Designed by Mr. R. Blake, Master Shipwright in H.M.'s Dockyards, 1806–1855.

Presented by the Rev. J. Hardie, Falmouth. 1866.

24. MODEL on "Blake's" plan of futtock to dispense with angle chock. Designed by Mr. R. Blake, Master Shipwright in H.M.'s Dockyards, 1806–1855.

Presented by the Rev. J. Hardie, Falmouth. 1866.

25. MODEL on "Blake's" plan of two floors made good with chocks at the side of keel. Designed by Mr. R. Blake, Master Shipwright in H.M.'s Dockyards, 1806–1855.

Presented by the Rev. J. Hardie, Falmouth. 1866.

26. MODEL of floor and first buttock united together on the old plan. Designed by Mr. R. Blake, Master Shipwright in H.M.'s Dockyards, 1806–1855.

Presented by the Rev. J. Hardie, Falmouth. 1866.

27. MODEL of common floor timber, chocked at the heel on the side of keel. Designed by Mr. R. Blake, Master Shipwright in H.M.'s Dockyards, 1806–1855.
Presented by the Rev. J. Hardie, Falmouth. 1866.

28. MODEL on "Blake's" plan of two bent floor timbers with saw-kerf in middle of moulding side, to assist the bending. Designed by Mr. R. Blake, Master Shipwright in H.M.'s Dockyards, 1806–1855.
Presented by the Rev. J. Hardie, Falmouth. 1866.

29. HALF BLOCK MODEL. Stern elevation of a three-deck line-of-battle ship. Wood construction. Starboard side, showing possible disposition of guns so as to obtain a nearly all-round and a right-aft line of fire.
Designed by Mr. R. Blake, Master Shipwright, H.M.'s Dockyards, 1806–1855.
Presented by Rev. J. Hardie, Falmouth. 1866.

30. WHOLE MODEL. Stern elevation of a three-deck line-of-battle ship. Wood construction.
Starboard side shows stern elevation completed.
Port side shows disposition of ship's timbers, wales, &c., and emplacement of gun ports for a right-aft and nearly all-round fire.
Designed by Mr. R. Blake, Master Shipwright, H.M.'s Dockyards, 1806-1855.
Presented by Rev. J. Hardie, Falmouth. 1866.

31. HALF BLOCK MODEL. Stern elevation of a three-deck line-of-battle ship. Wood construction. Starboard side, showing wales and plan of vertical timbering.
Mr. R. Blake, Master Shipwright, H.M.'s Dockyard, 1806–1855
Presented by Rev. J. Hardie, Falmouth. 1866.

32. HALF BLOCK MODEL. Stern elevation of a three-deck line-of-battle ship. Wood construction.
Starboard side showing wales, side timbering, and proposed stern disposition of timbers, ports, &c.
Designed by Mr. R. Blake, Master Shipwright, H.M.'s Dockyards, 1806–1855.
Presented by Rev. J. Hardie, Falmouth. 1866.

33. WHOLE MODEL of the bow of a frigate. Wood construction.

The upper portion of the model shows the bow of ship completed ; the lower part shows disposition and arrangement of timbers.
Starboard side on an old form ; port side on improved form of bow.
Designed by Mr. R. Blake, Master Shipwright, H.M.'s Dockyards, 1806-1855.
Presented by Rev. J. Hardie, Falmouth.   1866.

34. HALF BLOCK MODEL of the starboard bow of a three-deck line-of-battle ship, about 1835-1840. Wood construction, showing possible line of bow fire from four guns.
Mr. R. Blake, Master Shipwright, H.M.'s Dockyards, 1806-1855.
Presented by Rev. J. Hardie, Falmouth.   1866.

35. HALF BLOCK MODEL of the port bow of a three-deck line-of-battle ship. Wood construction. About 1840-1850, showing disposition so as to obtain a possible bow line of fire from six guns.
Designed by Mr. R. Blake, Master Shipwright, H.M.'s Dockyards, 1806-1855.
Presented by Rev. J. Hardie, Falmouth.   1866.

36. MODEL of an upper deck gun port, showing disposition of framing and timbers.
Designed by Mr. R. Blake, Master Shipwright, H.M.'s Dockyards, 1806-1855.
Presented by Rev. J. Hardie, Falmouth.   1866.

37. FIVE PIECES, Models, illustrating floor timbers for wooden ships.
Proposed by Mr. R. Blake, Master Shipwright, H.M.'s Dockyards, 1806-1855.
Presented by Rev. J. Hardie, Falmouth.   1866.

38. MODEL of the side of a ship of war, wood construction, showing side of lower deck port, and proposed method of re-sheathing an old ship below the water-line.
Proposed by Mr. R. Blake, Master Shipwright, H.M.'s Dockyards, 1806-1855.
Presented by Rev. J. Hardie, Falmouth.   1866.

39. THREE PIECES, Keel Blocks, Models.
Proposed by Mr. R. Blake, Master Shipwright, H.M.'s Dockyards, 1806-1855.
Presented by Rev. J. Hardie, Falmouth.   1866.

40. MODEL. Design for an improved head board for ships of war. Wood construction.
Proposed by Mr. R. Blake, Master Shipwright, H.M.'s Dockyards, 1806–1855.
Presented by Rev. J. Hardie, Falmouth.   1866.

41. EIGHT MODELS, illustrating various methods, old forms, and new proposals, for connecting beams to ships' sides. Wood construction.
Designed by Mr. R. Blake, Master Shipwright, H.M.'s Dockyards, 1806–1855.
Presented by Rev. J. Hardie, Falmouth.   1866.

42. WHOLE MODEL of a proposed and patented method for steam ship construction, designed by Dr. J. Collis Browne, late army medical staff.

> *Note.*—The ship is designed with a view of obtaining extraordinary buoyancy, increased speed and safety, freedom from pitching and scending. She is dry in the heaviest weather, and is a safety ship.
>
> The Model is fitted with a working screw propeller designed by Dr. J. Collis Browne, which is driven by model inverted screw engines, and copper boiler.
>
> Lent by Dr. J. Collis Browne.   1874.

43. WHOLE MODEL of a proposed screw steamship of new design by Captain Archibald Thompson, Liverpool.
The ship has channel ways on each side of the keel, running deep aft, and to nothing forward.
They form a water lead to the screw, which is placed forward well under ship's counter.
Lent by Mr. A. Thompson.   1874.
See also No. 71, page 133.

44. The contractor's MODEL actually used for the construction of the "GREAT. EASTERN" steamship, showing size and fittings, &c., of the Exterior iron plating.
Designed by the late Mr. I. K. Brunel, F.R.S.
Built by J. Scott Russell, F.R.S. This ship was designed in 1852, laid down in 1853, built 1857.
Lent by Mr. John Scott Russell, F.R.S.   1869.

45. The contractor's MODEL actually used for the construction of the "GREAT EASTERN" steamship, showing size and fittings, &c., of the Interior iron plating.
Lent by Mr. John Scott Russell, F.R.S.   1869.
> *Note.*—These Half-Block Models of the "GREAT EASTERN" are on a scale of ¼ in. to 1 foot.

46. Model of the construction of the Stern of the " Great Eastern " steamship.

Lent by Mr. John Scott Russell, F.R.S.   1869.

Note.—The " Great Eastern " steamship, originally called the " Leviathan," designed by the late I. K. Brunel, born 1806, died 1859, is the largest vessel afloat. She is propelled by paddle wheels as well as a screw propeller. The length of the " Great Eastern " is 680 ft. extreme, beam 83 ft., depth 58 ft. The ship has five decks, and was originally fitted up to carry 4,000 passengers, or when called on 10,000 troops. Tonnage 23,000 tons. Carries coals and cargo, 18,000 tons. Draught of water (light) 18 ft., draught of water (loaded) 28 ft. The ship has six masts, and is rigged partly square and partly fore and aft. She was built, and launched by hydraulic power, broadside on to the river Thames, at Mr. Scott Russell's works, Millwall. The "Great Eastern " is built of iron on Mr. Russell's wave-line principle, has a double bottom, affording ample and efficient space for water ballast, and is divided into compartments by water-tight bulkheads of iron. The paddle wheels are driven by engines on the oscillating-cylinder system of 1,000 horse power nominal. Each engine has two cylinders inclined inwards, and driving direct on the paddle shaft. Arrangements are made for disconnecting the engines from the wheels, or from each other. The engines form two separate and distinct double cylinder engines, having each their own air pumps, condensers, starting and stopping gear, &c. The diameter of the cylinders is 74 ins., length of stroke 14 ft., number of strokes per minute 14. Each cylinder is cast in one piece, and weighs 28 tons. The condenser is a casting in one piece weighing 36 tons. The upper frames of the engines are in four castings, each of 13 tons weight. The diameter of the paddle wheels is 58 feet, and in turning round once will advance 60 yards. The paddle engines (patented in 1853) and boilers were constructed by Messrs. J. Scott Russell and Company. The screw propeller is driven by horizontal direct acting engines on the connecting-rod principle, made by Messrs. James Watt and Company, Birmingham, and are of 1,700 nominal horse power. The engines have 4 cylinders, each 84 ins. diameter, and 4 ft. stroke. They drive a screw 24 ft. in diameter, 44 ft. pitch, and weighing 36 tons. The screw shaft is 160 ft. long and weighs 60 tons. The engines are controlled by Silver's patent marine engine governor, made by Hamilton and Co., Glasgow, 1859.

The boilers of the ship, 10 in number, supplied steam to the paddle wheel and screw engines at a pressure of 15 to 25 lbs. per square inch.

See Nos. 42 to 46, pp. 126, 127, also pp. 129, 130, 131.

47. Model showing Interior of a wooden merchant ship.

Lent by Lloyd's Register of British and Foreign Shipping, Cornhill.   1876.

48. MODEL showing the framing of the fore body of a wooden merchant ship.
Lent by Lloyd's Register of British and Foreign Shipping, Cornhill.   1876.

49. MODEL showing the framing of the after body of a wooden merchant ship.
Lent by Lloyd's Register of British and Foreign Shipping, Cornhill.   1876.

50. MODEL of a diagonally framed ship.   Thomas Bilbe's system of construction.—Composite.
Lent by Lloyd's Register of British and Foreign Shipping, Cornhill.   1876.

50. MODEL of a ship sheathed with diagonal doubling plank.   Sheathing according to Lloyd's rules, 1864.
Lent by Lloyd's Register of British and Foreign Shipping, Cornhill.   1876.

51. MODEL of Mr. John White's system of constructing composite iron and wood vessels.
Lent by Lloyd's Register of British and Foreign Shipping, Cornhill.   .   1876.

52. MODEL of an old ship showing framing, deck, beams, &c., also lower masts and bowsprit in place.
Lent by Lloyd's Register of British and Foreign Shipping, Cornhill.   1876.

53. Sectional MODEL of an iron vessel.
Lent by Lloyd's Register of British and Foreign Shipping.   '1876.

54. DRAWING of a composite vessel showing the iron framework, and the mode of fastening the wood bottom.
Lent by Lloyd's Register of British and Foreign Shipping, Cornhill.   1876.

55. DRAWINGS, 20, illustrating Lloyd's rules and regula- · tions for commercial shipbuilding on Mr. J. White's composite, or iron and wood system, and others.
Lent by Lloyd's Register of British and Foreign Shipping, Cornhill.   1876.

56. MODEL. Midship section of a composite vessel experimentally built and classed at Lloyd's for 11 years.
Lent by the Nelson Dock Company, Limited, Rotherhithe.   1876.

57. MODEL. Half midship section of a composite vessel experimentally built, and classed at Lloyd's for 15 years.
Lent by the Nelson Dock Company, Limited, Rotherhithe.   1876.

58. MODEL. Half model of an old paddle steamer.
Lent by the Nelson Dock Company, Limited, Rotherhithe.   1876.

59. MODEL. After body and stern framing of an old East Indiaman.
Lent by the Nelson Dock Company, Limited, Rotherhithe.   1876.

60. MODEL, midship section of a composite iron ship; showing timbers, keelsons, ribs and beams, diagonal bracing, and outside wood planking.
Lent by Messrs. Short Brothers, Shipbuilders, Sunderland.   1876.

61. MODEL, midship section of an iron composite ship; showing a proposed method for vertical iron plating and wood sheathing.
Lent by Messrs. Short Brothers, Shipbuilders, Sunderland.   1876.

62. MODEL, midship section of an iron composite ship; showing improved form of stringers and other detail of iron construction.
Lent by Messrs. Short Brothers, Shipbuilders, Sunderland.   1876.

Note.—With this model is another small model showing exterior wood planking and method of fastening it.

63. TWO WHOLE MODELS, illustrating framings in wood of old ships.
Lent by Mr. W. Roydon, Liverpool.   1876.

64. BLOCK MODELS showing lines and proportions of the "HIRSCH" ship. Designed by Hermann Hirsch, Craven Street, Strand, 1875.
Lent   1876.

Note.—The Models represent vessels of from 3 to 500 feet in length, and on this plan a steamship in the China trade, the "PAUNTING," 210 feet long, and 800 indicated horse-power, has already been built in 1873, by John Elder and Co., Glasgow. The peculiarity of the construction consists chiefly in forming channel ways along the line of

D 2

keel to secure less rolling propensity and afford efficient water supply to the screw propeller. A similar principle to the Hirsch ship has been designed for screw steamers by Captain A. Thompson of Liverpool, about 1873. See No. 43, p. 46.

65. PHOTOGRAPH of an old drawing representing the Twin-hull steamboat, "PRINCESS CHARLOTTE." Built in 1816 at Piehelsdorf near Spandau, Germany, by John Rubie and John Barnet Humphreys, English Engineers.

Lent by C. P. Rubie.   1876.

Note.—The " PRINCESS CHARLOTTE " double-hull steamer with one paddle wheel between them amidships, was built for the navigation of the rivers Elbe, Havel, and Spree. She began to run in November 1816, and was the first steamer put together or built in Germany. The engine of 14 horse-power was made by Messrs. Bolton and Watt. The drawing represents the ship as lying at " Die Zelten," Berlin. Her length was 130 feet 5 inches, width 19 feet 4 inches, tons 236 B.M.

66. MODELS made of Hard Paraffin for ascertaining the RESISTANCE OF SHIPS by measuring the Resistance of their Models.

Lent by Mr. W. Froude, F.R.S.   1876.

The models from 6 to 16 feet in length are made of Hard Paraffin. The experimental apparatus employed in working the model includes appliances for designing, moulding, and casting the models, shaping them by automatic machinery, moving them through the water at the required speeds, and automatically recording the leading phenomena of the trial, namely, the speed, the resistance, and the change of level induced by the speed at each end of the model.

The several processes are illustrated by the accompanying series of seven photographs and two specimens, which may be explained as follows :—

No. 1. The Designer.

This consists of a pile of adjustable templates, the thick-nesses of which represent the horizontal intervals between the successive water-lines of the intended models shown on a reduced scale. One edge of each template is an elastic steel band held to a wooden base-piece by adjustable ordinates hinged to the band and sliding through mortices in the base-piece fitted with hinged metal clamps. One of these templates (No. 8) set up as for use is sent to aid this explanation.

The photograph shows them in combination, and represents the intended small scale model by a series of water-lines in steps, which, if either filled up solid and fair to the salient angle of each, or trimmed off fair to the re-entering angle, would constitute the finished form.

No. 2. *a.* The Moulding Box; *b.* The Mould; and *c.* The Core.

Length. Breadth. Depth.
a. A rectangular wooden box 16′ × 2′ 9″ × 1′ 10″.

In this the external form of the full sized model (that is (*b*) the mould) is shaped by help of a series of rough cross sections deduced from the small scale designer, and into the mould is fitted the core (*c*), which constitutes the figure of the inside of the model. *c* is framed on a series of internal cross sections made good to a service and rendered coherent, first by a series of laths nailed to them externally, and, secondly, by a skin of calico drawn tight over the lathed surface, and then coated with plaster-of-paris and clay. Between this "core" and the "mould" there is, of course, a space, equal to the intended thickness of the model, into which space the melted paraffin is run, and there allowed to remain until by cooling it has become solid enough to bear removal.

Nos. 3 and 4, the Shaping Machine.

This is what has sometimes been termed in technical phrase a "copying machine." The model, bottom upwards, and adjusted successively to a series of different levels, travels longitudinally between a pair of revolving cutters, which are caused by means of a hand lever to so recede and approach one another, as the model passes, as to cut upon the model the horizontal section or "water-line," correctly appropriate to the level at which the model is set. At the side of the machine, in full view of the operator, there is a vertical board, which carries either a drawing of the intended model, showing the series of water-lines to be cut, or one of the "designer" templates already described. In front of this board is a "tracer," and the board and the tracer severally imitate upon the appropriate scales (the former by longitudinal motion, the latter by vertical motion) the longitudinal motion of the model and the lateral motion of the cutters. Thus the drawing (or template) passing along beneath the tracer is practically a small scale picture of the model travelling past the cutters, and if the tracer be made to follow the correct line on the drawing (or to follow the edge of the template) the revolving cutters will cut the correct water-line on the model.

The model is then finished by hand with spokeshaves and scrapers, an operation which takes a man about three hours.

No. 5. The Hauling Engine.

This is the instrument by which the required motion through the water at definite speed is given to the model. The dynamometric truck to which the model is attached is connected by a wire rope with a winding drum, driven by a small stationary double-cylinder steam engine. The engine is regulated by an extremely sensitive governor, acting upon a delicate steam throttle valve, on what is known as the "differential" principle, in which the governor rotates at its

own appropriate speed, independently of the engine, the
steam valve being opened or closed according as the engine
is lagging behind the governor or overtaking it.

By adjusting the centrifugal weights of the governor, with
a right and left-handed screw, and by differently speeding
the belt which connects it with the engine, any required
speed may be assigned to the engine between the limits of
about 150 and 350 revolutions per minute, and by further
changing the gear wheels connecting the engine and winding
drum, speeds varying from 60 to 1,200 feet per minute may
be assigned to the dynamometric truck.

Nos. 6 and 7. The Dynamometric Truck, with model under
it.

The dynamometric truck runs on a straight and level
railway about 200 feet in length, suspended over a waterway
36 feet wide and 10 feet deep. The model floating in the
water is as it were "harnessed" to the truck, and travels
with it. It is kept from diverging sideways by a knee-
jointed frame or "guider" at each end, of such construction
as to perfectly prevent the slightest sideways deviation of
the model, but in no way to interfere with its rising or falling,
or moving in a fore and aft direction with reference to the
truck. The towing strain (*i.e.*, the force necessary to make
the model accompany the truck in its longitudinal progress)
is taken during the experiment by a spiral spring, the extension of which, measuring the towing force, is indicated on
a large scale (through the intervention of certain levers) by a
pen which makes a line on a recording cylinder covered with
a sheet of paper. The recording cylinder is driven by the
truck wheels, and thus its circumferential travel indicates
distance run; at the same time another pen, jerked at half
second intervals by a clock, records time. Other pens
actuated by strings led over pulleys, record the change of
level of the ends of the model. Thus the diagrams made
furnish an exact measure of the speed, and a continuous
record of the resistances and of the change of level of the
model throughout the experimental run at steady speed.
While starting or stopping, the model is controlled by hand
levers to prevent the dynamometric spring being over-
strained.

No. 8. A " Designer " Template.

This consists of one of the pile of adjustable templates
shown in photograph No. 1, and already described.

No. 9. A Segment of a Model.

This specimen segment of a model is partly in a finished
condition and partly in the condition in which it is left by
the shaping machine, Nos. 3 and 4. It thus shows the series
of water-line cuts made by the machine, and a part of the
original cast surface remaining between the cuts.

CLASS IV.

Models of Fitments—Cabins and their fittings. Ports, Skylights, Hatchways, Ladders, &c.—Ventilation of Ships—Fire-hearths and Stoves.

1. MODEL of "Blake's" method for ventilating troop-ships.
Designed by Mr. R. Blake, Master Shipwright in H.M.'s Dockyards, 1806-1855.
Presented by the Rev. J. Hardie, Falmouth.   1866.

2. MODEL of "Blake's" plan for barring in the ports, and showing method of ventilation.
Designed by Mr. R. Blake, Master Shipwright in H.M.'s Dockyards, 1806-1855.
Presented by the Rev. J. Hardie, Falmouth.   1866.

3. "BLAKE'S" improved stopper bolt.
Designed by Mr. R. Blake, Master Shipwright in H.M.'s Dockyards, 1806-1866.
Presented by the Rev. J. Hardie, Falmouth.   1866.

4. SECTIONAL MODEL of a ship's side, showing proposed arrangement 'tween decks for the transport of troops. The model represents accommodation for about 20 men.
Designed by Mr. R. Blake, Master Shipwright, H.M.'s Dockyards, 1806-1855.
Presented by Rev. J. Hardie, Falmouth.   1866.

5. MODEL. Original design for horse stalls, as fitted at Malta, to the ships that conveyed the troops to the Crimea, 1854.
Lent by Mr. W. Ladd, Deptford Dockyard.   1864.

6. DRESSING CASE for ships' cabin. Japanese, modern.
From the London International Exhibition, 1874.
Presented   1875.

7. FIRE-HEARTHS or ships' Cooking stoves. Five Models, illustrating various plans for and arrangement of the above apparatus. Designed and fitted up in H.M.'s ships, royal yachts, &c., by Benham and Sons.
Lent by Messrs. Benham and Sons.   1869.

7—1. MODEL of ship's fire-hearth or cooking apparatus, 1-8th full size, fitted to H.M.'s Indian relief, steam screw troopships, by Benham and Sons. The hearth will cook and bake bread for 1,400 men.

7—2. MODEL of ship's fire-hearth or cooking apparatus fitted to ships of H.M.'s Navy and troop transport service. "Officers" fire-hearth, will cook and bake for 100 officers.

7—3. MODEL of circular ship's fire-hearth or cooking apparatus in a circular form, as fitted to the steamships of the Royal Mail West India Company. This hearth will cook and bake bread for 300 passengers.

7—4. MODEL of a ship's fire-hearth or cooking apparatus fitted to the steamships of the Peninsular and Oriental Company and of the Royal Mail West India Company. Ships' crews hearth, will cook and bake bread for 100 men.

7—5. MODEL of a ship's fire-hearth or cooking apparatus, fitted on board the steamships of the Peninsular and Oriental Company. The hearth will cook and bake bread for 200 passengers.

The above five models, lent by Messrs. Benham and Sons, Wigmore Street.   1869.

8. PATENT FIRE-HEARTH or cooking stove for yachts.
Lent by Messrs. Pascall Atkey, & Son, Cowes.   1874.

9. ORNAMENTAL STOVE for yacht's saloons and cabins.
Lent by Messrs. Pascall Atkey, & Son.   1874.
Note.—The cooking apparatus and cabin stove for yachts exhibited by Atkey and Son are used on board vessels belonging to the various yacht clubs of Great Britain. The cooking stove, 2 feet 2 inches long by 13 inches wide, will bake, boil, steam, stew, and roast, has a copper boiler for hot water, and plate and dish warmers.

10. MODEL on a scale of 3 ins. to 1 ft. of an ice house and cooling apparatus, fitted to the S.S. "CATHAY" and other steamships of the Peninsular and Oriental Company. The Model made by W. Denny and Brothers, Dumbarton.
Lent by the Peninsular and Oriental Steam Navigation Company, 122 Leadenhall Street, E.C.
1875.

11. COOKING DISHES.   (2)   "The   Magnet,"   "The "Universal."
Messrs. Kendall, Phillips and Co., Bristol.   1875.

12. TUBULAR ROASTING JACKS.   Brittens' Patent. (One 40 lbs., one 10 lbs.)
From the London International Exhibition, 1874.
1875.

13. GRIDIRON and TORMENTOR. Cooking utensils for ships' use.

From the London International Exhibition, 1874.

1875.

14. DRAWING (Lithograph), illustrating Prices's Patent Self-Trimming Hatchways for Steam Colliers. W. Denton, shipbuilder, Sunderland, agent.

Lent by Mr. W. Denton. 1876.

Note.—The Drawing represents a longitudinal through section of the screw steam collier, " J. B. EMINSON," built of iron at Sunderland. Scale $\frac{1}{8}$ in. to 1 ft. A midship section of the same collier loaded. Scale $\frac{1}{4}$ in. to 1 ft. Details of hatchways (side and end) for colliers ranging from 26 to 32 ft. beam.

CLASS V.

Appliances used in Ships.   Capstans and Windlasses. Tanks, Pumps, &c.   Anchors and Chain Cables, and gear connected with them.

---

1. THREE COMPRESSORS for chain cables. *a.* Original; *b.* As proposed by the Surveyor of the Navy, Sir William Symonds ; *c.* As proposed by the Plymouth-yard Officers. 1835.   1864.

2. DROGUE.˙ A canvass floating anchor about 2 feet square, used by fishing and other boats, to keep under weigh and head to sea.   ˙
Presented by Mr. C. W. Merrifield.   1869.

3. MODEL of " Blake's " slip hook for mooring chains. Designed by Mr. R. Blake, Master Shipwright in H.M.'s Dockyards, 1806–1855.
Presented by the Rev. J. Hardie, Falmouth.   1866.

4. MODEL showing " Blake's " stoppers for letting go anchors. Designed by Mr. R. Blake, Master Shipwright in H.M.'s Dockyards, 1806–1855.
Presented by the Rev. J. Hardie, Falmouth.   1866.

5. MODEL, snatch block, standard or pendant, for hauling in deep-sea lead lines. Designed by Mr. R. Blake, Master Shipwright, H.M.'s Dockyards, 1806–1855.
Presented by Rev. J. Hardie, Falmouth.   1866.

6. MODEL, wood, illustrating part of a proposed toggle. Designed by Mr. R. Blake, Master Shipwright, H.M.'s Dockyards, 1806–1855.
Presented by Rev. J. Hardie, Falmouth.   1866.

7. MODEL of a ship's bulwark, showing an improved method for stowing life buoys between the bulwark stanchions, along ship's side. Designed by Mr. H. S. Harland, Brompton, Scarborough.
Presented.   1874.

8. MODEL of the bows of an armour-plated ship-of-war, illustrating Martin's patent self-canting Anchors ; and their housing in board, etc. Also Models in Wood of Martin's chain cable links, with patent zig-zag welded joints.

Lent by Mr. C. Martin, 73, King William Street.

1874.

9. MODEL in silver.   Patent "stockless" Anchor. Small craft anchor.

Lent by Mr. Wasteneys Smith, C.E., Newcastle.

1876.

10. MODEL in brass.   Patent "stockless" Anchor.

Lent by Mr. Wasteneys Smith, C.E., Newcastle.

1876.

Note.—This anchor is said to possess—

1. Great holding power, with less weight, besides being diminished in the weight of the stock.

2. Extraordinary strength, proved at Lloyd's test.

3. It is always canted, no matter how it falls, and requires no stock to keep it canted.

4. Being always canted when on the ground, and by the assistance of the horns or toggles, it takes hold as soon as any strain is put upon the cable.

5. Spare, and wider, and different shaped arms for various grounds may be carried on board.

6. It will not foul or get fouled, and when holding there is nothing above ground, nor is there any stock to cause accidents.

7. It trips with great ease, because there is no stock to lift, and the crown end has so large a surface that good purchase is obtained for weighing.

8. It is easily fished, and can be stowed in-board on deck, thus clear of the bow, and avoiding risk of damage in case of collision of any description.

9. A ship may be speedily brought up by it, and ride with very short cable ; the steadying power being at the crown end, it is of no object if the shank is raised off the ground, which stocked anchors will not allow.

10. In shallow water no damage can occur to a ship's bottom, as no part of the anchor projects above ground.

11. It is at least one-third shorter than ordinary anchors, therefore soon clear of the water, and more convenient to manage.

12. It can be readily be disconnected, thus convenient to stow and easy to transport in case of need, its heaviest part being less than one-third its total weight.

13. It is made without welding, thus of great soundness.

14. It is worked with only one davit and tackle, therefore considering the saving of first cost and future maintenance of one davit and blocks, &c., it is by far the cheapest anchor to use, besides greatest safety and simplicity in working.

15. It is not dangerous when at "wash," for in the event of a collision the arms would simply be flattened to the ship's side instead of being driven in.

.6. Should the anchor be difficult or dangerous to weigh, from having got fast in rock or wreckage, a runner with messenger attached may bo slipped down the cable to the crown end, and by this means the anchor can be drawn out freely, as there are no barbs or palms to retard it.

17. Being of such greater strength and holding power, and requiring less cable than other anchors, shorter and stronger cables may be carried, thus increasing the safety of the ship without additional weight or cost.

Three Photographs representing Mr. Wastney Smith's "stockless" anchors, aground and slung, are hung in the Museum.

Presented.   1876.

11. MODEL of an Anchor invented by Sir Edward Belcher when a midshipman, 1815.

Lent by Admiral, the late, Sir Edward Belcher, K.C.B.   1876.

12. MODEL of a method of mending an anchor when the shank has been broken, 1830. The method is by means of three pieces of pig-iron.   ●

Lent by Admiral, the late, Sir Edward Belcher, K.C.B.   1876.

13. APPARATUS for distilling Fresh water from sea water. For use in ships' boats. Sharp and Smith's patent, 21, Eden Quay, Dublin, 1876.

Lent.   1877.

Note.—This little apparatus, made of copper and designed for supplying the crews of ships' boats with fresh water by distillation from sea water, consists of a boiler heated by parafine oil lamps. The steam from the salt water is carried off through a worm of pipe contained in a condensing chamber at the back of the lamp box. Cold water from the sea is conveyed through boats' side by a pipe to the condensing chamber which has an out-let pipe also running through boat's side. The apparatus exhibited consumes about $2\frac{1}{2}$ pints of oil in 18 hours, and will supply about three pints of fresh water per hour. The London agents for the apparatus are Sedgwick & Co., West Ferry Road, Millwall.

14. MAT for stopping holes in iron ships. Invented by Lieut. Makaroff, Imperial Russian Navy.

Lent by Creswell & Co., 140, Leadenhall Street, E.C. 1877.

Note.—These mats are used in the Russian Imperial Navy for stopping shot holes chiefly in iron-clad ships of war. A special drill for ship's company in using and securing these mats has been adopted. The mat is made of hempen fibre backed with canvas, and is saturated with tar.

CLASS VI.

Masts.   Rigging, standing and running.   Sails.

1. MODEL of the Masts, Rigging, and Sails, of H.M.S.
"GANGES." 84 guns. (On a ½-in. scale). Length 196 ft. 5½ in.,
breadth 52 ft. 2½ in., tonnage 2,285.   Laid down at Bombay
in 1819, launched in 1821.   Designed as "CANOPUS."
> Presented by the late Captain Hugh Talbot Burgoyne,
> R.N.   1865.

2. MODEL of section of a vessel with masts and sails
on the flat-surface principle.
> Presented by Lieut. W. Congalton, R.N.R.   1865.

3. Two MODELS of vessels illustrating a new method
of rigging ships with flat-surface sails.
> Proposed and lent by Lieut. W. Congalton, R.N.R.
>   1865.
> *Note.—a.* Model illustrating a merchant sailing ship, full
> rigged, of about 1,300 tons burthen.   Rigged to show masts
> and flat surface sails on Lieutenant Congalton's plan.
> *b.* Model illustrating the rig for a screw steamship,
> "Chinese fashion," with flat surface sails on Lieutenant
> Congalton's plan.

4. MODEL of Cunningham's self-reefing topsail, or
plan for reefing from the deck.   Invented by Henry D. P.
Cunningham, 1850.
> Lent by the late Mr. H. D. P. Cunningham.   1866.

5. MODEL, working of sails.   The upper deck of a
ship, showing two different arrangements of Cunningham's
patent method for reefing topsails from the deck.   The fore-
topsail and yard in the model is Cunningham's latest plan
and arrangement, 1870.   The main topsail and yard is the
original plan of Mr. Cunningham, 1850.
> Lent by the late Mr. H. D. P. Cunningham.   1871.

6. MODEL (same model as preceding) working of
yards.   The upper deck of a ship of three masts, fitted
with Cunningham's patent chain gear and windlass, for
hauling upon the braces of the lower yards, so as to square
or brace them by one operation.
> Lent by the late Mr. H. D. P. Cunningham.   1871.

7. Two MODELS of Studding Sails, with yards.   1864.

MASTS.

8. THREE MODELS of Faggot-built MASTS, for line-of-battle ships.
> Presented by Mr. J. S. Tucker. 1865.

9. MODEL of a patent Topmast, designed by Captain Turnbull.
> Presented by Messrs. Laurence Hill & Co., Glasgow.
> 1865.

10. MODEL. 4 pieces, painted; illustrating in wood Mr. R. Blake's plans for the construction and building up of the Masts of a ship of war, and showing dispositions of cheeks and outside pieces. Proposed by Mr. R. Blake, Master Shipwright H.M.'s Dockyards, 1806–1855.
> Presented by Rev. J. Hardie, Falmouth. 1866.

11. MODEL of the Mast of the Man-of-war "NELSON," in seven pieces, without the pieces which form the top.
> Lent by Mr. James Young, West Docks, South Shields. 1876.

DIMENSIONS, WEIGHT, AND EXPENSE OF THE "NELSON'S" MAIN MAST.

		£	s.	d.
No. 1.	Expense of seven trees -	- 860	16	6
2.	Hoops, bolts, and nails -	- 61	11	6
3.	Smith work - -	- 16	4	0
4.	Mast Makers - -	- 55	0	7¾
		993	12	7¾

		ft.	ins.
Length - -	-	- 127	2¼
Greatest diameter	-	- 0	41
Smallest diameter	-	- 0	30⅜

	Tons	cwt.	qrs.	lbs.
Weight - -	- 26	0	3	24

FITTINGS.

12. MODEL of "Blake's" single hook for futtock shrouds. Designed by Mr. R. Blake, Master Shipwright in H.M.'s Dockyards, 1806–1855.
> Presented by the Rev. J. Hardie, Falmouth. 1866.

13. TWO MODELS (*a* and *b*) of " Blake's "patent fids, and plans for fidding topmasts. Designed by Mr. R. Blake, Master Shipwright in H.M.'s Dockyards, 1806–1855.
Presented by the Rev. J. Hardie, Falmouth.   1866.

> *Note.*—One of these models (*b*) shows the fid plan adopted for the Royal Navy after trial on board H.M.S. " QUEEN," " S. VINCENT," " ILLUSTRIOUS," " WARSPITE," " VINDICTIVE," and others. 1807–1813.

14. MODEL of "Blake's" stoppers and fid for shortening the bowsprit. Designed by Mr. R. Blake, Master Shipwright in H.M.'s Dockyards, 1806–1855.
Presented by the Rev. J. Hardie, Falmouth.   1866.

15. MODEL of "Blake's" tumbler hook for letting go the sheet of a boat's sail in cases of emergency. Designed by Mr. R. Blake, Master Shipwright in H.M.'s Dockyards, 1806–1855.
Presented by the Rev. J. Hardie, Falmouth.   1866.

16. TWO MODELS, one iron and one wood, for steps of lower masts, on "Blake's" plan. Designed by Mr. R. Blake, Master Shipwright in H.M.'s Dockyards, 1806–1855.
Presented by the Rev. J. Hardie, Falmouth.   1866.

17. MODEL of "Blake's" plan, showing alteration in method of Securing Shrouds, and doing away with lower Deadeyes. Designed by Mr. R. Blake, Master Shipwright in H.M.'s Dockyards, 1806–1855.
Presented by the Rev. J. Hardie, Falmouth.   1866.

18. "Blake's" proposed DEADEYES for all ships. Designed by Mr. R. Blake, Master Shipwright in H.M.'s Dockyards, 1806–1855.
Presented by the Rev. J. Hardie, Falmouth.   1866.

19. Five plans (on "Blake's" principle) for TOGGLES. Designed by Mr. R. Blake, Master Shipwright in H.M.'s Dockyards, 1806–1855.
Presented by the Rev. J. Hardie, Falmouth.   1866.

20. SCREW EYE-BOLT (on "Blake's" plan). Designed by Mr. R. Blake, Master Shipwright in H.M.'s Dockyards, 1806–1855.
Presented by the Rev. J. Hardie, Falmouth.   1866.

21. MODEL in iron of a ratchet and lever for setting up ship's shrouds.   Designed by Mr. R. Blake, Master Shipwright, H.M.'s dockyards, 1806–1855.

Presented by Rev. J. Hardie, Falmouth.   1866.

BLOCKS.

22. (*a.*) One common Block, with hemp strop ; (*b.*) one with iron sheave, and seasoned wire strop, by Mr. Andrew Smith ; (*c.*) one iron bound block.   1864.

23. Common single Block.   1864.

24. Two common unfinished Blocks.   1864.

25. Two cheek Blocks.   1864.

26. Bound Block, with two side hooks.   1864.

27. Arnett and Co.'s patent roller Sheave, for ships' blocks.   1864.

ROPE.—HEMP AND FIBRE, IRON WIRE.

28. Specimen of Hemp Rope.   1864.

29. Specimen of Rope for hand and deep-sea lead.   1864.

30. Specimens of London made Hempen and Fibrous Rope for ships' rigging, tackle, and cordage.   " London staple."

Lent by Messrs. Frost, Brothers, Ropemakers, London Street, E.C.   1874.

Note.—The samples of hempen and fibrous rope exhibited by Frost Brothers, comprise the following descriptions :—

10-inch tarred hawser.   Manilla hemp.   Used generally in British vessels in preference to hawsers of other fibres.

8-inch white rope.   Manilla hemp.   Used for ships' hawsers by engineers and others.

9-inch four strand tarred rope.   Russian hemp.   Used for ships' standing rigging.

5½-inch four strand tarred rope.   Russian hemp.   Used for lanyards of large ships, and for yachts' rigging.

4½-inch cross spun tarred rope.   Manilla hemp.   A pliable rope and does not kink.

4½-inch cross spun white rope.   Manilla hemp.   A pliable rope and does not kink.

3-inch tarred rope. Manilla hemp. Used for ships'
running gear.
3½-inch four strand cable; laid white rope. Manilla
hemp. Used for dredging purposes.
3-inch four strand tarred rope. Russian hemp. Used for
yachts' gear.
Deep sea sounding line. Italian hemp.
Sounding line. Italian hemp. Used chiefly in telegraph
cable laying.
Lead line. Italian hemp.
15 thread log line. Italian hemp.
12 thread log line. Italian hemp.
Signal halyards. Italian hemp.
15 thread white hambroline. Italian hemp.
12 thread white hambroline. Italian hemp.
9 thread white hambroline. Italian hemp.
6 thread white hambroline. Italian hemp.
6 thread fine white hambroline. Italian hemp.
15 thread tarred hambroline. Russian hemp.
12 thread tarred hambroline. Russian hemp.
9 thread tarred hambroline. Russian hemp.
6 thread tarred hambroline. Russian hemp.
6 thread tarred hambroline. Russian hemp.

31. Collection of Rope and Cordage for ships' use.
Made by Thomas and William Smith, Newcastle-on-
Tyne.
Lent by Messrs. T. & W. Smith.   Newcastle, 1876.

Note.—This collection contains samples of iron wire rope
for standing rigging, with dead eyes seized in and spliced in.
Thimbles seized and spliced in. Heavy iron wire rope
4½ inches circumference; also hawser and rigging rope of
Manilla hemp. Deep sea lead lines, log lines, signal halyards,
house line, &c.

Specimens of tarred hemp rope ; for lanyards, ratlines,
wormed rigging, and tow ropes. There are also samples of
thimbles for lanyards; hanks for staysails : copper wire
rope and points for lightning conductors ; and other samples
of rope of galvanized iron wire.

32. Specimens of galvanized Iron wire and Rope, with
hearts for the same.   1864.

33. Specimens of Iron wire Rope, for standing rigging.
1864.

34. Specimens of Iron wire Rope,   1864.

35. Specimens of Iron wire and Copper wire Rope for ships' rigging, lightning conductors, &c.
Lent by Messrs. Newall & Co., London and Gateshead.
1874.

36. PIECE of BOLT ROPE, with two pieces of Canvas; used for parcelling. 1864.

37. SAMPLES of CANVAS used in the Royal Navy. Manufactured by Messrs. Baxter, Brothers, Dens Works, Dundee, 1876.
Lent 1877.

  Note.—The samples of canvas comprise—Sail canvas Nos. 1 to 6. 40 yards in the piece. Hemp sacking for coals, Royal Navy. Hammocking, Royal Navy. Duck, Royal Navy. Flax sheeting, Royal Navy.

CLASS VII.

**Methods of Propulsion.—Oars and Sculls.   Sweeps.
Steam Engines, Boilers, Screw propellers, Paddle
wheels, &c.**

MARINE STEAM ENGINES.

1. MODEL, on a scale of 1 inch to 1 foot, of the
horizontal condensing screw engines of H. M.'s turret ship,
" PRINCE ALBERT," 2,529 tons. Built 1864. 500 horse-power,
nominal.
> Lent by Messrs. Humphrys and Tennant, Engineers,
> Deptford.   1869.

2. MODEL, on a scale of 1½ inches to 1 foot, of the
horizontal condensing screw engines of H.M.'s turret ship
" MONARCH," 8,164 tons. Built 1868.   1,100 horse-power,
nominal.
> Lent by Messrs. Humphrys and Tennant, Engineers,
> Deptford.   1869.

3. MODEL, on a $\frac{1}{16}$th scale, of the horizontal condensing screw engines of H.M.'s ships, " NELSON," built 1814,
altered 1860 ; " CONQUEROR," built 1833, altered 1859 ;
"TAMAR," built 1863. 500 horse-power, nominal. Diameter of cylinders 71 inches. Stroke 3 feet.
> Lent by Messrs. Ravenhill, Easton, & Co., Engineers,
> Ratcliffe, E.   1869.

4. MODEL of the engines of the paddle-wheel steamer
" HELEN McGREGOR " of Liverpool. Designed and arranged
in 1843 by G. Forrester & Co., Engineers.
> Lent by Messrs. G. Forrester & Co., Liverpool.   1869.
> *Note.*—This engine has two inverted steam cylinders,
> a very long stroke, and occupies very little hull
> space. It is a condensing low-pressure engine,
> and is said to be still at work, 1873.

5. MODEL, on a scale of 1½ inch to a foot, of the
oscillating cylinder, paddle-wheel condensing engines of
the Holyhead and Kingstown Royal Irish mail steamer
" LEINSTER," 750 horse-power nominal. Diameter of cylinders 98 inches, stroke 6 ft. 6 inches.

To the engines are attached, on the same scale, the feathering float Paddle-wheels of the ship, the speed of which is about 21 statute miles per hour.
    Lent by Messrs. Ravenhill, Easton, & Co., Engineers.
                                                        1869.
    See Model No. 27, p. 15.

6. MODEL of a paddle marine engine, designed by J. Scott Russell, F.R.S., having three oscillating cylinders all connected to one crank on the paddle shaft. One of the cylinders is vertical, the other two are inclined inwards at about 45°.
    Lent by Mr. J. Scott Russell, F.R.S.   1869.
    The model made by Jabez James, Lambeth.

7. MODEL, working, on a 3 inch to 1 foot scale, of the vertical screw engines of steamship "A. LOPEZ," Cadiz and Havannah Spanish mail service.
    The engines are constructed on the hammer or inverted cylinder principle, and have condensers, air and feed pumps, variable expansion gear, &c. The model is a complete working condensing screw engine of about 20 horse-power. It was made in 1866–67, and exhibited in motion at the Paris Universal Exhibition of 1867.
        Messrs. W. Denny & Brothers, Engineers and Ship-
        builders, Dumbarton.   Purchased 1871.

8. SCREW ENGINES. High-pressure non-condensing screw engine of 3 horse-power; for screw steam yachts, Constructed on the hammer or inverted cylinder principle.
        Messrs. Verey & Lange, Engineers, late of Dover. 1874.
        See also Drawing of Messenger's patent steam boiler
        for yachts and launches, No. 30, p. 71.

9. SCREW ENGINE, full size steam engine for screw launches, or river pleasure yachts. Horse power.
        Lent by Messrs. Plenty & Sons, Newbury.   1874.

10. PHOTOGRAPH of Brotherhood and Hardingham's patent Three cylinder high-pressure horizontal steam engine, adapted for river screw pleasure yacht propulsion. The engine was designed and patented by Mr. P. Brotherhood, Engineer, in 1872–73.
        Presented by Messrs. Brotherhood & Hardingham,
        Engineers, Compton Street, London, E.C.   1874.

11. DRAWING on a 1 inch to 1 foot scale of the Inverted cylinder Compound screw engines of the screw steamships "WINDSOR CASTLE" and "EDINBURGH CASTLE," constructed in 1872 by Messrs. R. Napier and Sons. 270 horse power, nominal.

> Presented by Messrs. R. Napier and Sons, Glasgow.
> 1874.

12. MODEL IN WOOD.—Reversed Horizontal Marine Screw Engines. Built 1860.

> Lent by Messrs. J. and G. Rennie, Engineers, Holland Street, Blackfriars.   1876.

13. MODEL IN WOOD.—Horizontal Marine Screw Engines, with injection condensers. Made by J. and G. Rennie, 1860.

> Lent by Messrs. J. and G. Rennie, Engineers, Holland Street, Blackfriars.   1876.

14. MODEL IN WOOD.—Inverted cylinder Compound Engines of Peninsular and Oriental Company's ship "PERA." Indicated horse-power 2,000. Built 1872.

> Lent by Messrs. J. and G. Rennie, Engineers, Holland Street, Blackfriars.   1876.

> *Note.*—These engines for driving the screw propeller are on the upright or vertical system, and have surface condensers.

15. MODEL IN WOOD.—Screw engines of H.M. Ships · BOADICEA" and "BACCHANTE," on the compound system. 5,250 horse-power indicated. 1875 and 1876.

> Lent by. Messrs. J. and G. Rennie, Engineers, Holland Street, Blackfriars.   1876.

16. DRAWING. Design for 60 horse-power low pressure condensing Disc engine, for screw steam-ships.

> Lent by Messrs. J. and G. Rennie, Engineers, Holland Street, Blackfriars.   1876.

> *Note.*—The drawing shows front, side, and back elevation and plan of the Disc engine.
>
> Section of H.M.S. "CRUISER," fitted with the disc engine and comparing the space occupied by the old engines of the ship, 1853, which were of the same nominal horse power as the disc engine.

17. WORKING MODEL. Mr. Joseph Maudslay's original Oscillating cylinder Engines. Date 1827. (The arrangement for working the air pump is not that originally fitted.)

> Lent by Messrs. Maudslay, Sons, and Field, Engineers, Westminster Bridge Road.   1876.

18. SECTIONAL MODEL in wood, of side-by-side cylinder Horizontal compound Engines. John Milner, C.E., 1853. Lent by Mr. J. Warriner, per Messrs. Maudslay, Sons, and Field, Engineers, Westminster Bridge Road.   1876.

19. MODEL of Dawes and Holt's marine Screw Engine. Lent by Mr. Henry P. Holt, C.E., Leeds, and 4 Westminster Chambers, Victoria Street, S.W.   1876.

Note.—This is of the vertical compound condensing type, without intermediate receiver between high and low pressure cylinders, and very short passages, reverse action of pistons, parallel motion, single crank and connecting rod, one vertical and one horizontal air pump, the former forming a counterbalance to connecting rod, and the latter is arranged to be used as a starting cylinder when required.

20. MODEL of J. Ericsson's screw propeller Engines, applied to American and Swedish monitors.   Patented in America in 1858.

Lent   1876.

21. The ORIGINAL ENGINE of Henry Bell's steamboat " COMET," which was the first steamboat in Europe advertised for the conveyance of passengers and goods. 1812.

Lent.   1876.

Note.—This engine of 4-horse power nominal on the low pressure condensing system, has a single upright cylinder, and driving by means of connecting rods and side levers, the air pump and a single crank on the shaft on which is keyed a heavy fly wheel. It was made by John Robertson, mechanician, of Glasgow, and fitted on board the " COMET " in 1812. The paddles of the " COMET," four in number, were driven by gear wheels. Subsequently the boat was driven by two wheels only. The speed of the " COMET " was about [four miles per hour.

22. The ORIGINAL STEAM ENGINE made for Patrick Miller, Esq., by William Symington, Engineer, 1787, and used on the lake at Dalswinton, 1788.

Lent by Mr. Bennet Woodcroft, F.R.S.   1876.

Note.—For some years prior to 1787 Patrick Miller, Esq., of Dalswinton, Scotland, had been engaged in a series of experiments with double and triple vessels propelled by paddlewheels, worked by manual labour. In the experimental trips of 1786 and 1787 he was assisted by Mr. James Taylor (the tutor to his younger sons), and at the suggestion of the latter it was determined to substitute steam power for manual labour. For this purpose, in the year of 1788, Taylor introduced William Symington, an engineer at Wanlockhead Lead Mines, who had previously obtained letters patent (June 5, 1787, No. 1,610) for " his new invented steam engine on principles ' entirely new.' "

An arrangement was made with Symington to apply an engine constructed according to his invention to one of Mr. Miller's vessels, and consequently the engine which forms the subject of this notice was made, the castings being executed in brass by George Watt, founder, of Low Calton, Edinburgh, in 1788. At the beginning of October in that year the engine, mounted in a frame, was placed upon the deck of a double pleasure boat, 25 ft. long by 7 ft., and connected with two paddle-wheels, one forward and the other abaft the engine, in the space between the two hulls of the double boat. On the steam being put in action it propelled the vessel along Dalswinton Lake at the rate of 5 miles an hour.

23. MODEL of a direct-acting Marine Paddle Engine. Patented by J. Miller, 1841.

Lent   1876.

24. THREE DRAWINGS of the Inclined Cylinder Screw Engines of H. M.'s " CONSTANCE." Constructed in 1863 on the compound principle by Randolph Elder & Co., Engineers Glasgow.

Lent by John Elder & Co., Glasgow,   1876.

Note.—These engines were the first ever fitted in any of H. M.'s ships on the compound principle. Each engine has one high pressure cylinder of 60 inches diameter; and two low pressure cylinders of 78 inches diameter. The stroke is 3 feet 3 inches in length. The engines are fitted with surface condensers; air, bilge, and circulating pumps, and other modern arrangements. The drawings represent a plan of the engines, and two elevations of them as fitted in the ship, one looking forward, the other looking astern.

25. DRAWINGS. Compound Surface-Condensing Marine Engines.

Lent by Messrs. T. Richardson and Sons, Hartlepool, 1876.

Note.—Three drawings of marine engines of the most modern construction.

One drawing represents engines of the largest class from 250 horse-power nominal upwards, fitted with steam reversing gear, surface condensers, and other modern arrangements. Designed or constructed 1875.

Another drawing represents engines of a more moderate size, and gives the names of the vessels into which they have been fitted. Designed 1871-73.

A third drawing represents marine engines of the smaller class.

The three drawings all represent compound surface-condensing engines for driving the screw propeller. The engines were constructed from designs by Mr. Charles Smith.

26. DRAWING ; of a pair of Compound Marine Screw Engines ; inverted cylinders and all modern detail. Constructed by John Dickenson, Engineer, Sunderland.
Lent 1876.

BOILERS.

27. MODEL in wood, made in parts to take to pieces and show interior disposition. Marine multi-flue steam Boiler, Hawthorn's patent, 1868. Designed for high-pressure working, and with several new and special features, high furnaces, interior water tubes, high steam room.
Lent by R. & W. Hawthorn, Engineers, Newcastle.
1869

28. MODEL of a set of patent high-pressure Marine steam Boilers.
The boilers are designed for superheating the steam, heating the feed water, and having improved furnaces. Gray's patent.
Lent by Mr. Wm. Gray, Dawlish. 1874.
See No. 33, p. 72.

29. DRAWING, coloured, of a patented multi-flue Marine Boiler, by Messrs. R. & W. Hawthorn, 1868.
See Model of boiler, No. 27.
Lent by Messrs. R. & W. Hawthorn, Newcastle-on-Tyne. 1869.

30. DRAWING of Messenger's patent vertical water-tube Boiler for steam yachts and launches. Designed by Mr. Thomas Messenger, about 1869. Scale 3 inches to 1 foot.
Lent by the makers, Messrs. Verey & Lange, Engineers, late of Dover. 1874.
See also Screw-engines, No. 8, p. 67.

31. DRAWING on a $\frac{3}{4}$ inch to 1 foot scale of an improved marine water tube steam Boiler. Designed and patented by Messrs. J. and F. Howard, and made by the Barrow Shipbuilding Co., Barrow-in-Furness.
Lent by Messrs. J. and F. Howard, Engineers, Bedford.
1874.

32. DRAWING of Plenty and Sons patent horizontal high-pressure steam Boiler for screw launches for pleasure yachts.
Lent by Messrs. Plenty and Sons, Newbury. 1874.

33. DRAWING. Sections of Gray's patent high-pressure marine steam Boilers showing arrangement of the tubes, steam superheater, water heater, and flues.

Lent by Mr. W. Gray, Dawlish.   1874.

See also Model, No. 28, p. 71.

34. DRAWINGS, showing elevations, plans, and sections, of Dickenson's and Mace's Patent Multitubular Marine and Land Steam Boilers, 1876.   Constructed by J. Dickenson, Engineer, Sunderland.

Lent   1876.

35. DRAWING, showing part elevation, section, and plan, of the tubular Boilers of the paddle wheel steam yacht "GALATEA," 200, nominal horse power ; belonging to the Trinity House Corporation.

Lent by W. W. Willis.   1876.

36. DRAWINGS of marine steam Boilers for lecture purposes.   J. F. Flannery, Broadway Chambers, Westminster.

Lent   1876.

Note.—These drawings illustrate the boilers on the watertube system of Root and others, as fitted aboard the screw and paddle steamers " MONTANA," " PROPONTIS," " BIRKENHEAD," " GERTRUDE," &c., all of Liverpool.

37. ILLUSTRATIONS (full size) of the Connexions for the water tubes of marine steam water-tube Boilers.

Lent by Mr. J. F. Flannery, 6, Broadway Chambers, Westminster.   1876.

PROPELLERS.

38. THREE MODELS, showing the original design of the after bodies of the first screw steamers "ARCHIMEDES," built 1839 ; and "NOVELTY," built 1839–40.

The models show the forms of the original submerged screw propellers as fitted to the two ships, and modifications. The "NOVELTY" ultimately was driven by direct-acting engines and a two-bladed screw.

Also see No. 12, p. 36.

Lent by Mr. H. Wimshurst, Anerley.   1873.

39. MODEL No. 1, of a self-feathering screw Propeller adapted for auxiliary and small screw vessels, designed to obviate the necessity of raising the screw when under sail.

Proposed by the inventor and maker, Rev. P. A. Fothergill, Southend.   Lent, 1871.

40. MODEL No. 2, of Fothergill's self-feathering screw Propeller, adapted for auxiliary and small screw vessels, and obviating the necessity of raising the screw when under sail. The screw is entirely self-acting, requires no internal gearing. It can be set to any pitch, and used with any number of blades. See preceding Model.

Inventor and maker Rev. P. A. Fothergill, Southend.
Lent   1871.

41. MODEL of a double boat, fitted with a screw Propeller forward, to be driven by manual power; tried in Sussex river Ouse, 1823. The boat only attained a small rate of speed.

Lent by Mr. Burwood Godlee.   1872.

42. MODEL (unfinished) of ship construction, showing a peculiarly made propeller with three fans, also the plan for securing the same.   1846.   1864.

43. WHOLE MODEL of steamboat "JAMES LOWE," fitted in 1838 with a screw Propeller, under a patent granted to late Mr. James Lowe in March 1838, for "submerged propellers."

Note.—About the same time a large boat called the "WIZARD" was fitted with a screw or submerged propeller, under the late Mr. J. Lowe's patent.

Presented by Mrs. Henrietta Vansittart.   1874.

44. WHOLE MODEL of the steamship "GREAT BRITAIN," fitted on the late Mr. James Lowe's plan for submerged or screw Propellers, a patent for which was granted in March 1838.

Presented by Mrs. Henrietta Vansittart.   1874.

45. MODEL of the stern of a ship, fitted in March 1838 with a screw Propeller having one or more curved blades, sections or portions of a screw of uniform or increasing pitch, and placed below the water line of the ship.

Presented by Mrs. Henrietta Vansittart.   1874.

46. MODEL, in wood, of the first shaft and boss made for screw propellers, by late Mr. James Lowe, 1838.

Presented by Mrs. Henrietta Vansittart.   1874.

47. MODEL, in wood, of the first oval boss for screw propellers, made by Mr. James Lowe, 1855.

Presented by Mrs. Henrietta Vansittart.   1874.

48. MODEL, in wood, of the first spherical boss for screw propellers, made by Mr. James Lowe, 1852.
Presented by Mrs. Henrietta Vansittart. 1874.

49. MODEL, in gun metal, of a screw Propeller on the late Mr. James Lowe's principle for the blades, 1838.
Presented by Mrs. Henrietta Vansittart. 1874.

50. MODEL, in wood, on ¼-inch scale, of the " Lowe-Vansittart" screw propeller blades, as invented, and fitted in 1869 by Mrs. Henrietta Vansittart, for trial on board H.M.S. "DRUID," 350 horse power.
Presented by Mrs. Henrietta Vansittart. 1874.

51. DIAGRAM showing the original designs for submerged propellers and their blades, "Lowe's steamship propellers," patented 24th March 1838, by James Lowe. This diagram shows various proposals for the forms of blades of screw propellers.
Presented by Mrs. Henrietta Vansittart. 1874.

52. DIAGRAM illustrating Mr. James Lowe's proposals in 1855 for dividing the blades of screw propellers, and placing them in pairs or sets diagonally across the screw boss. Tried on board H.M.S. " BULLFINCH " in 1857.
Presented by Mrs. Henrietta Vansittart. 1874.

53. DIAGRAM of the modifications proposed in the "Wyche-Lowe" propeller blades, designed in 1852 by the late Mr. James Lowe, and tried on board the S.S. " MISKIN " and "ARGUS." Also the " Lowe-Harris " propeller. 1862.
Presented by Mrs. Henrietta Vansittart. 1874.

54. DIAGRAM of Mr. J. Lowe's fourth improvement in screw Propellers in 1862.
Presented by Mrs. Henrietta Vansittart. 1874.

55. DIAGRAM of a screw Propeller, and its blades, designed by Mrs. Henrietta Vansittart in 1868. Tried on board the Allan-line S.S. " SCANDINAVIAN," 400 horse power, in 1873, and H.M.S. "CADMUS," 21 guns, 400 horse power, in 1869. Known as the " Lowe-Vansittart " screw propeller.
Presented by Mrs. Henrietta Vansittart. 1874.

56. MODEL (full size) of a screw Propeller patented by Dr. J. Collis Browne, late Army Medical Staff.

Note.—The propeller is said to possess the following features :—

  a. Absence of vibration.
  b. Reduction of wear and tear in the driving machinery.
  c. Adaptability to any screw steamship.
  d. Facility for checking ships' way ; and for going full speed astern or ahead with increased speed and celerity.
  e. Direct action of the water on the axial line of screw.
  f. Affording increased steering power.

The steam screw river yacht " LAPWING," owner Dr. J. Collis Browne, is fitted with this screw, and on trial has given successful results.

Lent by Dr. J. Collis Browne, 34, Leadenhall Street, E.C. 1874.

57. WORKING MODEL in brass of Griffiths' screw Propeller, with screw gear, &c., for altering pitch of screw blades.

Lent by Mr. R. Griffiths, 1, Westmorland Road, Bayswater. 1875.

58. MODEL of Bevis's patent feathering screw Propeller.

Lent by Messrs. Laird Brothers, Engineers and Shipbuilders, Birkenhead. 1876.

Note.—Mr. R. R. Bevis, managing engineer to the firm of Messrs. Laird Brothers, of Birkenhead, in 1868 patented an arrangement for altering the pitch or feathering the blades of a screw propeller in a fore and aft direction, which claims to be a great advantage for screw steamers, making them faster and more handy when under sail alone, and when under steam and sail allowing of adjusting the pitch to obtain the best result. A screw propeller of the ordinary kind, whether fixed or revolving, is a heavy drag against speed and handiness for sailing, and " lifting " it is a laborious operation, and requires a large hole or well through the ship's counter to admit of so doing.

The arrangement of this new screw propeller is free from many of the objections which have been made to feathering screws previously tried. The gear for feathering the blades is well protected, the levers and other gear that move the blades being enclosed within the boss of the screw propeller, and attached to a rod passing through the centre of the shaft, which is worked in the screw shaft funnel. This system is admirably adapted for ships of war or sailing ships with auxiliary power, or yachts, where it is as important to have a good result under sail alone as under steam. The operation of altering the pitch, or of feathering the blades to any angle, is done in a few minutes, without in any way putting the engines into a position that they may not be used in an emergency.

59. MODEL of a Propeller for ships.

Lent by Mr. S. F. Pischler, London.   1876.

Note.—The model represents a propeller designed to have a motion similar to that of an oar used at the stern of a boat in sculling.

60. DRAWING, coloured; of a method proposed by Messrs. E. J. Reed, C.B., and H. Wimshurst, for raising and lowering the screw propeller of steam ships, according to their draught of water. Proposed 1875–76.

Lent by H. Wimshurst.   1876.

61. DRAWING of the original screw Propeller; designed by the late Mr. G. Rennie about 1840, and tried in H.M.'s Iron Ship "DWARF," the first screw steamer in the Royal Navy.

Lent by Messrs. J. and G. Rennie, Engineers, Black-
          friars.   1876

Note.—The "DWARF" was tried in May 1843 and attained a speed of 12 miles per hour. There is an exact model in brass of this screw propeller also lent by Messrs. J. and G. Rennie.

See No. 41, page 19.

62. MODEL in brass of the screw Propeller designed by the late Mr. G. Rennie about 1840, for H.M.'s Iron Ship "DWARF."

Lent by Messrs. J. and G. Rennie, Engineers, Black-
          friars.   1876.

Note.—This screw was tried in May 1843 in H.M.S. "DWARF" and drove the vessel at a speed of 12 miles per hour. She was the first screw steamer belonging to H.M.'s Navy, and was originally called the "MERMAID."

See also No. 41, page 19.

63. SKELETON MODEL of part of a vessel fitted with a screw Propeller. (Cummerow's patent, 1828.)

Lent by Mr. Bennet Woodcroft, F.R.S.   1876.

Note.—This idea of a screw propeller was communicated in 1828 from abroad to Charles Cummerow, who took out letters patent. The original drawings of this invention show the propeller applied at the bow and stern of different vessels, and also placed between two boats fastened .together. The propeller in the model consists of one whole turn of a screw.

64. MODEL in wood of the late Sir Francis Petit Smith's double screw Propeller, patented 1836.
Lent by Mr. B. Woodcroft, F.R.S.   1876.

65. MODEL of vessel fitted with screw propeller, by the late Sir Francis Pettit Smith, 1836.
Lent by Mr. Bennet Woodcroft, F.R.S.   1876.

Note.—The propeller consists of two whole turns of a screw thread round its shaft, and is placed in the dead wood or run of the vessel, but by a memorandum of alteration the patentee limits himself to a screw of one turn or two half turns.

66. THREE MODELS in wood, showing the Forms from which the blades of screw-propellers are obtained.
Lent by Mr. B. Woodcroft, F.R.S.   1876.

67. MODEL in wood. Increasing-pitch screw propeller. Bennet Woodcroft, 1832–1846.
Lent by Mr. Bennet Woodcroft, F.R.S.   1876.

68. VARYING-PITCH SCREW PROPELLER on shaft.
Lent by Mr. Bennet Woodcroft, F.R.S.   1876.

Note.—The first varying-pitch screw propeller ever made was designed by Mr. B. Woodcroft in 1844 in which year he obtained Letters Patent. In 1845 this description of screw was submitted to the Admiralty. In 1846 a full sized screw was made of gun metal by Sir Joseph Whitworth, Manchester, for H.M.S. "DWARF." This screw was 5 feet 8 inches in diameter. The angle which the two blades will form with the shaft may be altered so as to give a pitch ranging from $4\frac{3}{4}$ feet to $10\frac{3}{4}$ feet.

69. THREE MODELS of Sterns of Vessels fitted with screw Propellers of varying pitch. Woodcroft's patent, 1844.
Lent by Mr. Bennet Woodcroft, F.R.S.   1876.

Note.—With one of these models is exhibited a single blade of these screw propellers showing its isolated form.

70. MODEL in brass fitted to the stern of a ship. Varying-pitch screw Propeller. 'Designed by Mr. B. Woodcroft, F.R.S., 1844.
Lent.   1876.

71. MODEL in brass fitted to the stern of a ship Varying-pitch screw Propeller. Designed by Mr. B. Woodcroft, F.R.S., 1844.
Lent   1876.

Note.—The blades of this screw, two in number, are cut from a screw with an increasing pitch.

· **72.** MODEL in brass fitted to the stern of a ship. Varying-pitch screw Propeller. Designed by Mr. B. Woodcroft, F.R.S., 1844.
Lent   1876.

Note.—This screw propeller has four blades.

73. ORIGINAL MODEL. Vessel constructed by Bennet Woodcroft for experiments on propulsion with paddlewheels and screw propellers, 1832–1846.
Lent by Mr. B. Woodcroft, F.R.S.   . 1876.

74. MODEL of a PADDLE WHEEL with improved Floats. Designed about 1850.
Lent by Mr. B. Woodcroft, F.R.S.   1876.

STEAM ENGINE AND BOILER ACCESSORIES.

75. OBJECTS lent by Messrs. Schäffer & Budenberg, 1, Southgate Street, St. Mary Street, Manchester.   1874.

1. 5-inch Pearson's patent lubricator.

2. Mercury vacuum gauge.

3. Thermometer.

4. Bourdon's patent pressure gauges. Steam and vacuum.

5. Schaeffer's patent pressure gauges. Steam and vacuum, with diaphragm springs.

6. Counter, 7 figure, with resetting key. For counting revolutions of engines, &c.

76. SALINOMETER ; How's Patent, for measuring the quantity of sea salt in marine steam boilers.
Lent and made by Mr. T. O. Buss, Hatton Garden.
1874.

Note.— In using the Salinometer the water drawn from the boiler should be at 200° Fahrenheit ; the instrument is adjusted for this temperature.—It is graduated from 0· to 4·32. 0′ Fresh water. 1·32 sea water, which contains 1 lb. of salt to 32 lb. of water. 2·32 indicates 2 lb. of salt to 32 lb. of water ; and so on.

To keep a marine boiler clean, the water should not contain more than 2 lb. salt to 32 lb. water.

77. PHOTOGRAPH of a steam Donkey Engine and pump for feeding steam boilers with water. The pumps are single and double acting.

Presented by the makers, Messrs. Brotherhood & Hardingham, Engineers, Compton Street, E.C. 1874.

78. STEAM DONKEY ENGINE and pump, single acting for feeding steam boilers with water.

Lent by makers, Messrs. Alexander Wilson & Co., Engineers, Vauxhall Works, Wandsworth Road, S.
1871.

79. SERIES of MODELS in brass of Governors for land and marine steam engines, and other inventions. Thomas Silver, Philadelphia, U.S.A.

Lent. 1876.

Note.—These governors designed by Thomas Silver of Philadelphia are intended principally for controlling the marine engines of screw steamships and preventing what is technically known as "racing." They were adopted for use by the British Admiralty in 1869.

80. BOILER PLATE two specimens, bent and broken, to show the quality of the iron.—(A.) Atlas iron plate, (B.) best iron plate for boilers.

From the Atlas Steel and Iron Works, Sheffield. 1864.

CLASS VIII.

Steering Apparatus. Rudders, permanent and temporary. Steering gear of all kinds, Manual and Steam.

1. MODEL of R. Napier & Sons' patent screw steering gear, fitted to the French Mail Atlantic steam ship " CITY OF PARIS," screw, and now usually fitted by them to large ocean steam ships.

Presented by R. Napier & Sons, Glasgow.   1867.

2. MODEL of a double Rudder fitted to stern of a screw steamer. Proposed by Lieut. the Hon. J. Fitzmaurice, R.N.

Lent by Lieut. the Hon. J. Fitmaurice, R.N.   1865.

3. MODEL of a balance Rudder.

Proposed and presented by Mr. J. S. Tucker.   1865.

4. MODEL of the stern of a ship fitted with J. Scott Tucker's proposed balance Rudder, which can only be unshipped when at right angles with the keel.

Presented by Mr. J. S. Tucker.   1865.

5. MODEL of a flat-bottomed schooner, with an outside Tiller. About 1820.

Presented by Mr. J. S. Tucker.   1865.

6. WORKING MODEL of a ship's steering wheel known as the " Niagra " wheel, because fitted on board the United States corvette, " NIAGARA." Designed 1857.

Lent by Mr. Andrew Murray, Chief Engineer, Portsmouth Dockyard.   1867.

> *Note.*—The rudder head is suspended on friction rollers, and the screw gear to move the rudder is of special mechanical arrangement.   •

7. MODEL balance rudder and arrangement of stern for twinscrew steamships (iron built). Proposed by Mr. C. W. Merrifield, F.R.S.

Lent by Mr. C W. Merrifield, F.R.S.   1869.

8. THREE MODELS showing various systems of " Lumley's" patent rudder.

Invented by H. Lumley, Assoc. I.N.A.

Lent.   1865.

9. MODEL, illustrating Admiral E. A. Inglefield, C.B. invention. The "Hydrostatic" steering apparatus, for heavy ships. The model shows the method adopted in fitting the apparatus to Her Majesty's ship "ACHILLES," 6,000 tons, 1,250 horse-power.

Lent by Admiral E. A. Inglefield, R.N., C.B., F.R.S.
1871.

Note.—Her Majesty's ship "ACHILLES," iron, 20 guns' 1,250 horse-power, armour plated screw, ship. Length 380 ft., breadth 58 ft. 3½ in., depth 21 ft. 1½ in., tonnage 6,121. Laid down at Chatham Yard in August 1861 in a dock, undocked in December 1863. Designed by the Controller's Department, Admiralty, on lines very similiar to Her Majesty's ships "WARRIOR" and "BLACK PRINCE," built in 1860.

The armament is as follows :—

	No.	Prs.
Main deck	$\begin{cases} 8 - \\ 8 - \end{cases}$	- 100-pr. 6½-ton guns. - 6½-ton rifled guns.
Upper „ -	- 4 -	- 6½-ton „
	20	

Her complement of men, 705.

10. MODEL of a proposed Steering apparatus, 1861.
1864.

11. MODEL of " Blake's " plan for adding power to the rudders of gunboats, and vessels of light draught. Designed by Mr. R. Blake, Master Shipwright in H.M.'s Dockyards. 1806–1855.

Presented by the Rev. J. Hardie, Falmouth.　　1866.

12. MODEL of "Blake's" plan for constructing a temporary rudder. Designed by Mr. R. Blake, Master Shipwright in H.M.'s Dockyards, 1806–1855.

Presented by the Rev. J. Hardie, Falmouth.　　1866.

13. MODEL of the rudder of a ship of war, wood construction, showing arrangement and scarfing of the timbers, disposition of the braces, rudder head, and other portions.

Designed by Mr. R. Blake, Master Shipwright, H.M.'s Dockyards, 1806–1855.

Presented by Rev. J. Hardie, Falmouth.　　1866.

F 2

14. Model of the stern of a screw frigate showing Admiral Martin's plan (1858) for Steering apparatus, arranged to work the rudder-head clear of the screw well.

1864.

Note.—The tiller, tiller-ropes, &c. all work on the starboard quarter.

15. MODEL of the Bridges used on board H.M.S. "ORONTES" and others, for carrying and launching ships' life-boats.

Lent by Mr. John White, Medina Docks, Cowes.

1876.

Note.—This is a working model of Mr. J. White's plan, adopted by the Admiralty for H.M. ships of war and Indian relief troop ships, for carrying and launching life-boats from ships' upper deck.

The life-boats are carried athwart ships on a rocking bridge originally designed by Messrs. Hire and White. Arrangements are made for openings in ships' bulwarks to allow either end of the rocking bridge fall down to the edge of ships' upper deck. This gives sufficient inclination to launch the boat either way first. The rocking bridge when canted forms the launching ways.

16. MODEL of bow of vessel, showing bow Rudder, with guard on. Patent taken out by the late Mr. John Laird in 1843.

Lent by Messrs. Laird Brothers, Engineers and Shipbuilders, Birkenhead. 1876.

Note.—Very generally adopted for all double-ended river steamers, and fitted in several paddle-wheel gun vessels.

CLASS IX.

Boats :—Ships' Boats. Life Boats and Rafts. All kinds of Boats and Barges used for pleasure.

---

1. WHOLE MODEL of the Australian Life-boat "LADY DALY" built at Adelaide, from design by Mr. W. Taylor, Government Shipwright at that port, about 1867. Length 43 ft. 1 in.; breadth 9 ft.; depth midships 4 ft. 1 in. Scale ¾-inch to 1 foot. The model was presented to His Royal Highness the Duke of Edinburgh, by the Marine Board of South Australia in 1868.

Lent by His Royal Highness the Duke of Edinburgh.

1869.

See also Drawing, No. 67, p. 132.

2. MODEL of the Boat built by exhibitors (in 1861) for use of Her Majesty the Queen, and His Royal Highness the Prince Consort, during their visit to Ireland and Lake of Killarney in 1861. The boat was built for Lord Castlerosse. Scale ⅜-inch to 1 foot.

Lent by Searle and Sons, Lambeth.   1872.

3. FOUR MODELS of ships' Boats built of steel, with screw propellers, and fitted with engines designed especially by John Penn, Esq., F.R.S., of Greenwich. The boats are planned out for the ships of war, designed by the late Vice-Admiral E. P. Halsted, R.N., in 1866. Each carries two guns forward, protected by moveable iron breast-plates.

Presented by R. Napier & Sons, Glasgow.   1867.

1. *Launch.*

Length	-	-	- 50 feet.
Guns -	-	-	- 2 ten-pounders.
Oars -	-	-	- 22

2. *Pinnace.*

Length	-	-	- 45 feet.
Guns -	-	-	- 2 ten-pounders.
Oars -	-	-	- 20

3. *First Cutter.*

Length	-	-	- 35 feet.
Guns -	-	-	- 2 two-pounders.
Oars -	-	-	- 14

4. *Second Cutter.*

Length   -   -   - 30 feet.
Guns -   -   -   - 2 two-pounders.
Oars -   -   -   - 12
See also No. 5, p. 8 ; No. 8, p. 23 ; No. 14,
p. 37 ; No. 3, p. 97 ; Nos. 16 and 17, p. 101.

4. SECTION, full size, showing portion of strake and
gunwale of steel boats, with metal crutch. ·
Designed by the late Vice-Admiral E. P. Halsted, R.N.,
in 1866.
Presented by R. Napier & Sons, Glasgow.   1867.

5. STATE BARGE, built at Deptford ; length 45 ft.,
beam 6 ft. 7 in. Has a covered state cabin abaft, and pulls
with twelve oars. Built 1702–1707, George Prince of
Denmark, Lord High Admiral of England.
Lent by the Admiralty.   1869.
Note.—This barge has been removed to Greenwich
Hospital.

6. MODEL of H.M.'s steam troopship "ORONTES," on a
¼-scale ; showing the arrangement of three canting bridges
for life-boats, with life-boats built on Lamb and White's
principle. Also ten of Captain J. W. Hurst's patent life
rafts, lashed to ship's sides.
Lent by Mr. J. White, Cowes.   1873.

7. SERIES of MODELS (nine in number) of Life-boats,
built on Lamb and White's principle. Originally designed
in 1846 for the Peninsular and Oriental Steam Navigation
Company, and since used on board Her Majesty's steam
yachts, "VICTORIA AND ALBERT," built 1855. - "OSBORNE,"
built 1843. "FAIRY," built 1854. - "ALBERTA," built 1863.
"ELGIN," built 1849.
These life-boats are also adopted for Her Majesty's Navy,
and the Coast Guard and Trinity House services.
Lent by Messrs. J. White & Co., Cowes, Isle of Wight.
1873.

7—1. Model, on about ¾-inch scale of a life-boat state
barge. Presented by the Peninsular and Oriental Steam
Navigation Company in 1857 to the Bey of Tunis.

7—2. Model, on about ¾-inch scale, of the "MARY WHITE"
life-boat. Presented to the boatmen of Broadstairs by Mr.
Thomas White of Cowes. Used in rescuing the crew of
the ship "NORTHERN BELL" off Kingsgate in January 1857.

7—3. Model of a life-boat on about ¾-inch scale, as furnished
to Her Majesty's ships and services. 1846.

7—4. Model of 36 ft. life-boat, originally designed in 1846, for the Peninsular and Oriental Steam Navigation Company, and now used on board Her Majesty's ships and transports.

7—5. Model of a life-boat barge, pulling fourteen oars, used in Her Majesty's services. 1859–60.

7—6. Model of the coast-guard life-boat, ordered to be built, and tried in Dingle Bay, Ireland, in 1864, and now (1873) the pattern boat for coast-guard service round England, Ireland, and Scotland.

7—7. Model of a yacht's gig fitted as a life-boat. 1872.

7—8. Model of a yacht's life boat adopted by the Royal Yacht Squadron, New Thames Yacht, and other yachting clubs of the kingdom.

7—9. Model, on about a ¾-scale, of the construction, arrangement, and fitting of a life-boat built on Messrs. Lamb and White's principle. 1871.

The port side of Model shows disposition of boat's frame and planking.

The starboard side fore bow shows the boat as finished ; after end shows the water-tight lining and planking.

The above nine models lent by Mr. J. White, Cowes. 1873.

8. NINE MODELS of Life-boats, ships' boats and others. Lent by Messrs. J. Bond and Son, Norway Yard, Limehouse, late Forrest and Son, Limehouse. 1873.

8—1. Whale life-boat, for H.M's ship " SYLVIA." Length 28 ft., beam 5 ft. 8 in., depth 2 ft. 6 in., ¾-inch scale.

8—2. Life-boat cutter for H.M.'s ship "SYLVIA." Length 25 ft., beam 7 ft. 3 in., depth 2 ft. 10 in., ½-inch scale.

8—3. Self-righting cutter life-boat, for H.M.'s navy. Length 28 ft., beam 7 ft. 6 in., depth 3 ft. 2 in., ½-inch scale.

8—4. Life-boat for Trinity Corporation's screw steamer " VESTAL." Length 25 ft., beam 6 ft., depth 2 ft. 4 in., ¾-inch scale.

8—5. Canoe surf-boat for West Coast of Africa. Length 31 ft., beam 6 ft., depth 2 ft. 4 in., ¾-inch scale.

8—6. Unsinkable steam launch for ships' and yachts' use. Length 26 ft., beam 6 ft. 6 in., depth 3 ft. 3 in., ¾-inch scale.

8—7. Special hospital surf-boat for service on West Coast of Africa. New design by Messrs. Forrest and Son, for War Department. Scale 1 inch to 1 foot, length 25 ft., depth 2 ft. 3 in., breadth 5 ft.

8—8. The yawl " KATE," owner E. E. Middleton, who

sailed her alone, all round England in 1869. Scale 1 inch
to 1 foot, length 23 ft., breadth 7 ft., depth, 2 ft. 6 in.

8—9. South Sea whale boat, on a 1 inch to 1 foot scale,
length 30 ft. 6 in., breadth 5 ft., depth 2 ft.
Lent by J. Bond and Sons, late Messrs. Forrest & Sons.
1873.

9. MODEL of the LIFE-BOAT and its transporting Carriage, on about a $\frac{1}{10}$th scale; adopted by the Royal National
Life-boat Institution, 14, John Street, Adelphi, London.
Designed for the Institution by Mr. Joseph Prowse in
1861.

Note.—The form of this boat is that usually given
to a whale boat with a long flat floor amidships,
sides straight, raking stem and stern post, diagonally
built of two thicknesses of mahogany and copper
fastened. Length, extreme, 33 feet; breadth of beam,
8 feet, and depth inside, 3 feet 4 inches. The boat
has five thwarts 2 feet 8 inches apart, and pulls 10 oars
double-banked in crutches formed on the thole pin.
Extra buoyancy is obtained by the compartments
under the deck being filled with water-tight cases
packed with cork, detached air cases under the head
and stern sheets, and along the sides under the
thwarts, and the end air cases in the extremes. It
is not probable that this boat could be readily upset,
but should such an accident occur provision is made
by the sheer of gunwale, raised air cases in the
extremes, weight of cork in the bottom, and the iron
keel to cause her to right herself. The area of the
delivering valves will enable the boat to readily free
herself of all water above the deck in 20 seconds,
with 47 persons on board.

This life-boat possesses in the highest degree all the
qualities which it is desirable that a life-boat should
possess, viz., great lateral stability, speed against a
heavy sea, facility for launching and taking the shore,
immediate self-discharge of any water breaking into
it. The advantage of self-righting if upset, strength,
and stowage room for a number of passengers.

The carriage consists of a fore and main body. The
latter is formed of a keelway, and of side or bilgeways attached to the keelway, and resting on the main
axle, the boat's weight being entirely on the rollers of
the keelway. Its leading characteristic is that, on
the withdrawal of a forelock pin, the fore and main
bodies can be detached from each other. The advan-

tages of this arrangement are, that whilst the weight
of the boat, when she is launched from the rear end,
forms an inclined plane by elevating the keelway, to
replace her on the carriage she can be hauled bow
foremost up the fore end or longer incline. The
bilgeways are needed at the rear end, that the boat
may be launched in an upright position with her crew
on board, but they are not required at the fore end
of the carriage. The boat is hauled off the carriage
and launched into the sea by ropes rove through
sheeves at the rear end of the carriage, each having
one end hooked to a self-detaching hook at the boat's
stern, and the other manned by a few persons on the
shore, who thus haul the boat and her crew off the
carriage and launch them afloat at once, with their
oars in their hands ; by these means headway may
be obtained before the breakers have time to beat the
boat broadside on to the beach.

Lent by the Royal National Life-boat Institution.
                                                1865.

10. MODEL. Life-boat. Length 36 ft., breadth 7 ft. 10 in.
Designed and lent by Mr. George Turner, late Master
Shipwright, Woolwich Dockyard.   1864.

11. MODEL. Life-boat. Length 26 ft.
Proposed and lent by Mr. George Turner, late Master
Shipwright, Woolwich Dockyard.   1864.

12. MODEL of a Life-boat, designed in 1854. Length
32 ft., breadth 8 ft. 4 in. Scale ¾-in. to 1 foot.
Proposed by Mr. D. Harvey.   1865.
Note.—This Model has been removed to Greenwich Hospital.

13. MODEL. Illustrating a mode of fitting Boats, either
singly or in couples, for the disembarkation of troops,
horses, and field-guns. This plan was used in the landing
of troops in the Crimea, 1854–1856.
Lent by the inventor, Mr. W. Ladd, Deptford Dockyard.   1864.

14. MODEL of Berthon's patent collapsible troop Boats.

Length	- - -	50 feet.
Beam	- - -	14 feet.
Depth	- - -	6 feet 3 inches.
Oars	- -	12
Troops	- -	200

Designed and lent by the Rev. E. L. Berthon, Romsey,
Hants.   1867.
Note.—There are two models of these boats exhibited :
one expanded for use, and the other "collapsed" or shut up
for stowing.

15. Two MODELS showing "Fawcus's" new mode of constructing Boats, so that several of the same size and shape may be packed together indiscriminately.
Lent by Mr. G. Fawcus, North Shields.   1866.

16. MODEL of a ship's bulwark fitted with "Fawcus's" patent revolving head Davits, for lowering and stowing boats promptly.
Lent by Mr. George Fawcus, North Shields.   1866.

17. Two BLOCKS. "Fawcus's" improved blocks for lowering ships' boats, with necessary fittings for boat's side, thwarts, &c.
Presented by Mr. George Fawcus, North Shields.
1865.

18. Two MODELS showing arrangements of boat-chocks with sliding wedge pieces, on Mr. Fawcus's plan.
Lent by Mr. George Fawcus, North Shields.   1866.

19. MODEL of Captain Hurst's patent bulwark life Raft, complete.
Lent by Captain J. W. Hurst, M.M.   1868.

20. MODEL showing mode of fitting Hurst's patent bulwark life Raft to waist-bulwarks of a ship.
Lent by Captain J. W. Hurst, M.M.   1868.

21. YOKE and CRUTCHES, made from a brass gun taken in Sebastopol, 8th September 1855. Presented to the late Capt. Crispin, R.N.
Lent by Mrs. Crispin.   1865.

22. WORKING MODEL of Clifford's patent Boat-lowering apparatus.
Lent by Mr. A. Battan, Northumberland Alley, E.C.
1874.

Note.—One man performs the operations of unlashing, lowering, and releasing the boat, which cannot cant to one side, nor can one end of the boat enter the water sooner than the other. The boat can be lowered whilst the ship is at full speed, and when she quits the ship steerage way is left, which enables the coxswain to keep her away clear from ship's side. .

23. MODEL of the eight-oared "Outrigger," built for the Cambridge University crew in 1860. Length 58 ft., breadth 2 ft. 2 in., depth 1 ft. 1½ in.
Built and lent by Messrs. Searle & Sons, Lambeth. 1865.

24. MODEL, on 1-in. scale, of the last State Barge built in 1807 for the Lord Mayors of London.

    Lent by Messrs. Searle & Sons, Lambeth   1865.

    Note.—See also No. 80, p. 134 ; No. 4 and 4a, p. 103.

25. MODEL of an Ice Boat, such as is employed on the Gulf of Finland, the Canadian lakes, &c. The length of the " SOKOL " (FALCON) is about 25 ft., and at her widest part, where the mast rises, she is 12 ft. broad.

    Presented by Mr. John S. Anderson.   1865.

26. WHOLE MODEL of an improved and patented Life-boat, designed by Dr. J. Collis Browne, late Army Medical Staff.

    Note.—The boat possesses it is said :—

      a. Extraordinary buoyancy. She affords shelter in the fore and aft projections, to the rescued.

      b. She rides easily in the heaviest sea.

      c. She can be worked to windward by oars alone.

    Lent by Dr. J. Collis Browne.   1874.

27. WORKING MODEL of Dr. J. Collis Browne's patented method for Lowering ships' boats at sea by means of his patent clip hooks, which release both ends of the boat simultaneously, although one end of the boat take the water first.

    Lent by Dr. J. Collis Browne.   1874.

28. CLIP HOOKS, patent. A pair, full size, of Dr. J. Collis Browne's patent clip hooks for letting go ships' boats at sea.

    Lent by Dr. J. Collis Browne, 34, Leadenhall Street, E.C.   1874.

29. WORKING MODEL of Hill's patent Boat lowering apparatus. Pair of slip hooks, full size. [Messrs. Hill & Clark.]

    Lent by Mr. E. J. Hill, 6, Westminster Chambers, Victoria Street, S.W.   1874.

30. WORKING MODEL of a Boat lowering apparatus, designed by R. J. Fairbridge.

    Presented by Mr. R. J. Fairbridge, 57, Neville Road, Stoke Newington, N.   1875.

    Note.—The covers for these boats are also specially prepared to serve for stopping leaks, &c.

31. DOLBY's patent water-bottle life Buoys.

    Thomas G. H. Dolby, 22, Camberwell Green.   1875.

32. MODELS of Life-saving apparatus (a boat and raft).
Designed by C. Robert.
From the London International Exhibition, 1874.
1875.

33. MODEL of Sweeting's patent Boat lowering apparatus
with life-boat attached.
F. J. Sweeting, Clyde Dock, Rotherhithe.   1875.

34. MODEL of life Raft. Designed by Lieut. R. J. Rowe,
R.N.   1875.

35. MODEL of a Shields pilot Coble.
Lent by Mr. James Young, West Docks, South
Shields.   1876.

CLASS X.

Instruments for Navigation :—Compasses, Logs, Chronometers, Sextants, &c., Barometers. Nautachometers, Clinometers, &c. Signal Flags, and Ships' Lights.

---

1. Berthon's patent NAUTACHOMETER or perpetual log, for indicating speed of ships.
Lent by the Rev. E. L. Berthon, Romsey, Hants. 1867.

2. Berthon's patent bi-fluid CLINOMETER, for showing the oscillation, pitching, and scending of ships, and also their trim.
Lent by the Rev. E. L. Berthon, Romsey, Hants. 1867.

COMPASSES.

3. TWO MODELS of ship's binnacles. Proposed for the Navy, 19th March 1853, as an improvement on the square box then in use. Scale 3 in. to 1 foot.
Mr. D. Harvey.   1865.

Note.—These Models are removed to Greenwich Hospital.

4. SHIP'S COMPASS and BINNACLE. Gray's patent.
Lent by Mr. John Gray, 26, Strand Street, Liverpool.
1877.

5. SHIP'S COMPASS. Self-registering compass. Mr. J. M. Napier's patent.
Lent by D. Napier & Sons, Lambeth.   1874.

6. GIMBOL COMPASS for yachts and small craft.
Lent by Mr. H. Sandham.   1875.

LOGS.

7. SHIPS' LOGS. Two patent rotating brass logs, with self-acting mile indices and registers, arranged on Massey's principle.
Manufactured and lent by Mr. L. P. Casella, Holborn.
1874.

Note.—These frictionless propeller logs are of two sorts; one is the older form with a square end or tail, while the other has the improved conical end or tail which prevents the liability of the former to jump out of the water when towed at high speed. Both these logs are made on Massey's patented principles.

8. Massey's patent SHIP'S LOG, with mile indices to register the distance run.

> Lent by Mr. Edward Massey, 17, Chadwell Street, Clerkenwell, E.C. 1876.

Note.—This log is one of Mr. Massey's original patents for ships' logs which register constantly the distance run by ships. The logs consists of two parts, one being the rotator or actual log, which is attached to the second part, the mile indices. The rotator in dragging through the water revolves and drives by wheel-work the indices which register permanently the number of miles run.

9. Massey's Patent Frictionless Propeller LOG with conical end.

> Lent by Mr. Edward Massey, 17, Chadwell Street, Clerkenwell, E.C. 1876.

Note.—This log is designed with a view of overcoming the many faults found in practice to exist in the preceding description of log No. 8. The frictionless propeller log is formed in one piece instead of two distinct parts. The rotation of it is insured by the vanes at the after end, and this rotation drives the indices which registers permanently the distance run. The conical end of this log does away with all suction from the end, and the liability of jumping from the water in quick sailing is prevented.

10. Massey's patent Hand Lead and deep sea SOUNDING MACHINE.

> Lent by Mr. Edward Massey, 17, Chadwell Street, Clerkenwell, E.C. 1876.

Note.—This machine consists of two parts : 1, the lead, much of the usual shape, and 2, the index of the number of fathoms passed by the lead. This index has a screw propeller which forced through the water by the weight of the falling lead rives an index showing evolutions of the screw. The rotator or screw propeller makes four revolutions in passing through one fathom of water, so that for the number of fathoms the instrument has passed through there will be an equivalent number of revolutions of the rotator, which are indicated by the graduated scales of the register. The rotator is held fixed in its place by a shield which both for casting and hauling in, prevents any further action of the screw either before or after the sounding.

11. Massey's patent SOUNDER. An instrument for registering depth in fathoms.

> Lent by Mr. Edward Massey, 17, Chadwell Street, Clerkenwell, E.C. 1876.

Note.—This instrument is self-contained in one piece. The rotator or screw which drives the index in passing through the water is protected by a ring guard. The index is divided into fathoms and registers 120 to set which, turn the nut on index cover until the word "set" on it is brought to the centre opposite the pointer. In hauling in the rotator is set fast to prevent any further action.

12. The "PENDENT LOG," patented.

Lent by Messrs. Cohen, Jacob, & Co., agents, Ely Place and Charterhouse Street, Holborn.   1876.

Note.—This log is formed of two parts, one called the rotator, which is the log proper, in the form of a screw, and the other called the register which gives the number of knots traversed by the ship while the log is thrown out and in action. The apparatus is intended to be used permanently, and should be attached to ships's quarter rather than her stern in order to keep the rotator more out of ship's wake.

SHIPS' LIGHTS.

13. SET OF STEAM SHIP'S LIGHTS.   Three.

1 port light.

1 starboard light.

1 anchor or masthead light.

The lanterns of copper.

Lent by Messrs. Stevens & Sons, Southwark Bridge Road.   1874.

14. TWO SHIP'S SIGNAL LANTERNS, copper. Arranged so as to form with one lantern, a starboard, port, or white riding light. (1869.) The lanterns are of two sizes, the larger fixes on a stand and revolves, and can be used probably for "flashing," and signalling.

Lent by Mr. J. S. Starnes, Broad Street, Ratcliff.
1873.

15. SIGNAL LANTERN, or Riding light.   Captain Colomb's R.N. riding light, fitted with improved light apparatus and lantern glass or lense, for increasing the brilliancy of the light.

Lent by Capt. Colomb, R.N.   1873.

16. A set of ships' SIGNAL LIGHTS and cabin lamps on the "Silber" light system. These lights and lamps comprise ships' starboard, port, and riding lights, signal lights and lamps for saloon and cabin use.

Lent and manufactured by the Silber Light Co., 49, Whitecross Street, E.C.   1877.

17. Fog-horn. To be blown by bellows.
Lent by Mr. J. S. Starnes, Broad Street, Ratcliff. 1873.

18. "Anderson Fog Alarm," or Horn. The Anderson Fog Alarm and Manufacturing Company, New York.
From the London International Exhibition, 1874.
Presented 1875.

Note.—Patented July 1868 and August 1871; adopted by the United States Government, July 1871.

19. Case containing Four Distress Signal Rockets.
1. Shows red light and explodes with loud report.
2. Explodes with loud report.
3. Discharges a shower of red stars.
4. Crimson detonating signal light.
Messrs. Brock and Co., Nunhead Green, Peckham.
1875.

20. Holmes' Shipwreck Distress Signal Flare and Life Buoy Rescue Lights.

Note.—These have the remarkable property of bursting into flame when placed in contact with water, and when once ignited are absolutely inextinguishable by either wind or water. They emit a most powerful white light, as brilliant as the magnesium light, and continue to burn over 30 minutes. The shipwreck distress signal flare is visible on a dark night with a clear atmosphere at a sufficient elevation for over ten nautical miles, and burns with greater brilliancy the more seas sweep over it.

The light is a chemical light, and produced by the action of the water upon phosphuret of calcium, giving off phosphuret of hydrogen, which, combining with the oxygen in the atmosphere, spontaneously ignites. These distress signals are free from danger, are not affected by heat, friction, or percussion, and contain no explosive compound whatever.

Lent by Mr. N. J. Holmes, 8, Great Winchester Street Buildings, E.C. 1876.

21. Holmes' Mechanical Compound Reed Fog Horn.
Lent by Mr. N. J. Holmes, 8, Great Winchester Street Buildings, E.C. 1876.

Note.—These mechanical fog alarms are constructed upon the most approved acoustical principles, and emit a most powerful sound. The "aurora" fog horn can be heard over three nautical miles, and the note produced is the 8 foot C of the musical scale. The tone is produced by the vibrations of two metal tongues, placed together in absolute contact, and closing the same reed, by which means (the split tongue) a powerful vibration is set up with a minimum pressure of air. The air bellows consist of two metal cylinders, one working inside the other; and the compressed air upon the return of the cylinder is driven through the reed into an inner trumpet-shaped tube contained within and a part of the external cylinder.

CHRONOMETERS.

22. CHRONOMETERS, 8 and 2 day marine chronometers. Fitted complete. Also the movements only.
> Lent by Victor Kullberg, 105, Liverpool Road, Islington, N. 1874.

23. SHIPS' CHRONOMETER (2 day). Fitted complete for ships' use.
> Lent by Messrs. Charles Frodsham and Co., 84, Strand. 1876.

24. CHRONOMETER BALANCE. Cut open—for action under heat and cold. Ordinary construction without auxiliary.
> Lent by Messrs. James Poole & Co., Spencer Street, Clerkenwell. 1876.

25. CHRONOMETER BALANCE, in rough state from casting.
> Lent by Messrs. James Poole & Co., Spenser Street, Clerkenwell. 1876.

26. ENGLISH KEYLESS WINDING MECHANISM. Modern specimens of workmanship for fuzee and going barrel. ¾ plate lever and pocket chronometer Movements.
> Lent by Messrs. James Poole & Co., Spenser Street, Clerkenwell. 1876.

27. SHIP CHRONOMETER (2 day), complete. This chronometer has an auxiliary compensation balance.
> Lent by Messrs. James Poole & Co., Spenser Street, Clerkenwell. 1876.

28. SHIP CHRONOMETER (2 day). Movement reversed, to show workmanship.
> Lent by Messrs. James Poole & Co., Spenser Street, Clerkenwell. 1876.

CLASS XI.

Guns :—Breech and Muzzle-loading Guns.   Shot and
    Shell.   Batteries, Turrets, &c.

₊ *The Objects in this Class have been chiefly transferred to the
Collection of Munitions of War, and are there exhibited.*

1. MODEL of 7-in. breech-loading, naval pattern,
"Armstrong" Rifled Gun complete, with sights and vent
piece. Manufactured at the Gun Factory, Royal Arsenal,
Woolwich, 1867.   .   .   ·   Purchased 1867.

2. SERIES of ILLUSTRATIONS of GUNS and PROJECTILES
adopted in the Royal Navy, 1866–67. Known 1874, as
"Armstrong" and "Woolwich" systems for rifled ordnance.
From the Royal Arsenal, Woolwich.   Purchased 1867.

    1. Model of a 7-inch breech-loading Armstrong gun,
    with sights and vent piece complete. Manufactured at the
    Gun Factory, Royal Arsenal, Woolwich.
    2. Wood model of a 7-inch muzzle-loading, wrought-iron,
    Woolwich rifled naval gun.

SHOT AND SHELL.

    3. 13-inch mortar shell, whole.
    4. 13-inch mortar shell in section, filled and fused.
    5. 10-inch carcass, whole.
    6. 150-pr. smooth-bore naval shell.
    7. 68-pr., grape shot, Caffin's pattern.
    8. 68-pr., solid shot.
    9. 7-inch shot for Armstrong's breech-loading gun.
    10. 7-inch common shell for Armstrong's breech-
loading gun.
    11. 7-inch common shell in section, empty.
    12. 7-inch segment shell for Armstrong's breech-loading
gun.   .   •
    13. 7-inch segment shell in section, filled, with adapter
and Boxer's 9 seconds wood time fuze for rifled ordnance.
    14. 7-inch segment shell in section, empty, unleaded.
    15. 64-pr. hollow-headed shot, for breech-loading Arm-
strong gun.
    16. 8-inch diaphragm shrapnel shell, for smooth-bore
guns.
    17. 8-inch diaphragm shrapnel shell, in section, filled,
and Boxer's diaphragm wood time fuze.
    18. 8-inch diaphragm shrapnel shell in section, empty.
    19. 8-inch naval shell, whole.
    20. 8-inch naval shell in section, empty.
    21. 8-inch Martin's shell, whole.

22. 8-inch Martin's shell in section, showing the filling with molten iron.

23. 12-pr. solid shot.

24. 12-pr. howitzer case shot.

25. 12-pr. segment shell for Armstrong's breech-loading gun.

26. 12-pr. segment shell for Armstrong's breech-loading gun, in section, filled, Dyer's field service percussion, and Armstrong time fuze.

27. Hand grenade for sea service.

28. 12-pr. Congreve rocket and stick complete.

29. 12-pr. Congreve rocket in section.

30. Lubricator for 7-inch breech-loading Armstrong gun, complete, and in section.

31. 8-inch junk wad, used for firing hot shot.

32. 8-inch grummet wad.

METAL FUZES.

33. Boxer's time fuze, 20 seconds, for naval service whole, in section filled, and empty.

34. Boxer's time fuze, 7½ seconds, for naval service, whole, in section filled, and empty.

35. Armstrong time fuze, for breech-loading guns, whole, in section filled, and empty.

36. Armstrong pillar percussion fuze, for breech-loading guns, whole, in section filled, and empty.

37. Petman's percussion fuze, for naval service, whole, in section filled, and empty.

38. Petman's percussion fuze, for land service, whole, in section filled, and empty.

39. Dyer's field service percussion fuze, whole, in section filled, and empty.

WOOD FUZES.

40. Mortar fuze, large, whole, and in section filled.

41. Mortar fuze, small, whole, and in section filled.

42. Boxer's wood time fuze, 9 seconds, for breech-loading Armstrong guns, whole, and in section filled.

43. Boxer's wood time fuze, 2-inch common, whole, and in section filled.

44. Boxer's wood time fuze, diaphragm shrapnel, whole, and in section filled.

45. Wood fuze for hand grenades.

3. SERIES of MODELS and PROJECTILES, contributed by the Whitworth Armoury Company (Limited), Manchester, showing Sir Joseph Whitworth, Bart., system for rifled guns and projectiles, ranging in calibres from a 2-pr. to a 9-in. or 320-pr. rifled gun.

Proposed for Vice-Admiral Halsted's system of turret and broadside ships of war. 1867.

See Models of Ships, No. 5, p. 8.

3. Projectiles designed by Sir Joseph Whitworth, Bart., 1867.

1. Longitudinal section of a 3-pr. Whitworth bore, with elongated shell, and rifled sphere, to illustrate the rotation of projectile.
2. 9-inch Whitworth shell, length 45 inches, weight , for firing at close action.
3. 9-inch Whitworth steel shell, length 26 inches, weight, empty, 310 lbs., bursting charge 10 lbs., total 320 lbs.
4. 9-inch rifled sphere.
5. 7-inch Whitworth steel shell, weight 150 lbs., bursting charge 6 lbs.
6. 7-inch shrapnel shell, in section.
7. 7-inch case shot, in section.
8. 7-inch rifled sphere, weight 43·75 lbs.
9. 70-pr. Whitworth shot.
10. 70-pr. rifled sphere, weight 21 lbs.
11. 70-pr. shrapnel shell.
12. 70-pr. shrapnel shell, in section.
13. 70-pr. case shot.
14. 70-pr. case shot, in section.
15. 32-pr. Whitworth shot.
16. 32-pr. rifled sphere, weight 9 lbs.
17. 32-pr. shrapnel shell.
18. 32-pr. shrapnel shell, in section.
19. 32-pr. case shot.
20. 32-pr. case shot, in section.
21. 10-pr. Whitworth shot.
22. 10-pr. rifled sphere.
23. 10-pr. common shell.
24. 10-pr. shrapnel shell.
25. 10-pr. shrapnel shell, in section.
26. 10-pr. case shot.
27. 10-pr. case-shot, in section.
28. 2-pr. common shell.
29. 2-pr. case shot.
30. 2-pr. case shot, in section.
31. 2-pr. rifled sphere.
32. 1-pr. Whitworth steel shot.
33. 1-pr. Whitworth steel shot, with ogival head.
34. 1-pr. Whitworth steel shell.
35. Whitworth tubular cartridge for 9-inch gun, charge 45 lbs.
36. Cross section of Whitworth 7-inch bore, and 7-inch shot, fitted on stand, for the purpose of showing the windage.
37. Small iron plate ½-inch in thickness, showing two penetrations of steel shot, fired at an angle with the Whitworth rifle.

4. WHOLE MODEL of a twin screw gun-boat, fitted to show method of working the Gun turret by chain and winch gear, the patented system of the exhibitor.

Lent by the late Mr. H. P. D. Cunningham, Gosport.

1872.

5. MODEL of the broadside battery of a ship of war, showing four Guns arranged to work by steam power from the deck below the gun deck. The driving drum being kept going, when the different gun ropes are pulled upon, motion is at once given to the guns; on slackening the ropes the motion ceases.

Proposed by the late Mr. H. P. D. Cunningham, Gosport.
Lent. 1872.

6. MODEL of a broadside battery of a ship of war, showing one Gun, designed to be worked from the deck below the gun deck, by means of a revolving shaft, pullies, and sheaves. An endless chain running over these, runs the gun in and out. Revolving bollards in rear part of gun slide, kept in motion by above gear, enables the gun to be traversed in either direction by pulling on the gun ropes when cast round the bollards.

Proposed by the late Mr. H. P. D. Cunningham, Gosport.
Lent. 1872.

7. MODEL of the broadside battery of a ship of war, showing two Guns. The right-hand gun illustrates the traversing gear for the first 12-ton naval gun used on board H.M.S. "EXCELLENT" in 1866, for traversing heavy guns by one man. H.M.S. "MINOTAUR" was fitted on a modified system of the above, for four years.

The same gun in the model also illustrates the method of running in and out of 12-ton guns, used for four years on board H.M.S. "EXCELLENT" and "MINOTAUR."

The left-hand gun shows a proposed plan (1862) for loading the gun in-board; also a slide block compressor, applied to the first 110-pr. Armstrong gun on board H.M.S. "EXCELLENT," 1865. In use two years.

The pivot-bar is shown in the model placed under instead of upon the gun port sill. This method is adopted in the Royal Navy.

Proposed by the late Mr. H. P. D. Cunningham, Gosport.
Lent. 1872.

8. MODEL in wood of a wrought-iron gun carriage Platform. Fitted with Cunningham's patent Bollards, for controlling and working the gun.

Lent by the late Mr. H. P. D. Cunningham, Gosport.

1872.

9. MODEL in wood, on a scale of 1½ inch to 1 foot, illustrating a plan designed by Mr. Cunningham for working Heavy. Guns in ships' turrets by steam power. The steam is led up through the hollow point on which the turret revolves, to a steam cylinder placed in the centre of the gun slide. The end of the piston rod is fixed to the gun carriage. The gun is run in and out by working the steam valve lever. The steam cylinder can be also used to check recoil. The model further illustrates a plan for raising or lowering the gun at the trunnions to obtain extreme elevation or depression. A plan similar to the model has been applied to the turret Guns of H.M.S. "HERCULES" and "GLATTON."

Lent by Mrs. Cunningham.   1875.

10. MODEL of a Forecastle of a ship of war, fitted; showing Pivots, Racers, &c., to enable the guns and carriages to be shifted from one position to another for firing in any direction.

Purchased from Royal Arsenal, Woolwich.   1867.

1. Model, gun carriage, naval pattern, sliding, for 7-inch breech-loading gun.

2. Model, gun carriage, naval pattern, sliding, for 7-inch muzzle-loading gun.

3. Model, gun carriage, naval pattern, for 32-pr. gun, muzzle-loading, old pattern.

4. Model of a gun carriage, common naval pattern.

5. Model, slide, for 32-pr. gun.

6. Model, slide, for 7-inch breech-loading gun.

7. Model, slide, for 7-inch muzzle-loading gun.

Set of Models of small stores for above :—
  (a.) Dismounting chocks.
  (b.) Transporting axles with trucks.
  (c.) Roller handspikes.
  (d.) Wad hook.
  (e.) Rammers.
  (f.) Sponges.
  (g.) Levers (traversing).
  (h.) Levers, lifting joints, &c.
  (i.) Ramps for raising carriages on to slides.

11. MODEL of a Mortar Bed, complete, showing the method adopted (1866) for fitting it to the deck of a ship of war so as to obtain an all-round fire. Together with a Model in wood of a 13-inch sea service Mortar, mounted.

Purchased from Royal Arsenal, Woolwich.   1867.

12. MODEL, showing section of a boat with two Guns, and apparatus for working them, on Mr. Walker's plan.
Lent by Mr. J. Walker. 1867.

13. MODEL of a 3-gun Battery, showing the working of the guns on Mr. Walker's plan.
Lent by Mr. J. Walker. 1867.

14. MODEL of a floating Battery of 3 guns, on Mr. J. Walker's plan. Lent by Mr. J. Walker. 1867.

15. MODEL of a gun-boat.
Presented by Mr. J. S. Tucker. 1865.

16. MODEL, showing portion containing three Guns, of main deck Battery of the late Vice-Admiral E. P. Halsted's combined turret and broadside ships of war. Designed, 1866.
Presented by Messrs. R. Napier & Sons, Glasgow. 1867.
Note.—The guns are mounted upon iron carriages, designed by Captain T. B. Heathorn, R.A., on his system for muzzle pivoting.
See No. 5, page 8, and No. 3, page 97.

17. MODEL, a complete working model of R. Napier's patent Turret designed to contain two "Whitworth" rifled 9-inch Guns; and adopted for the combined turret and broadside armour-plated ships of war, proposed by the late Vice-Admiral E. P. Halsted, R.N., in 1866.
Note.—This model shows the steam turret revolving gear between decks, the method of supporting the turret, the upper and lower decks of ship, and internally the mounting and emplacement of the guns in the turret.
Presented by Messrs. R. Napier & Sons, Glasgow. 1867.
See Models, No. 5, page 8; No. 14, page 37; No. 18, page 42; No. 3, page 83; No. 3, page 97.

18. MODEL, in brass, of an Old pattern naval service muzzle-loading smooth-bore Gun.
Presented by Rev. J. Hardie, Falmouth. 1866.

19. MODEL. Gun fitted, on the inside principle, to H.M.S. "RAPID." Naval service. 1864.

20. MODEL. Two Guns on the common principle. Naval service. 1836. 1864.

21. MODEL. Mode of fitting a 32-pounder Gun of 25 cwt. in H.M.S. "IMOGEN." Portsmouth Yard, 1831. 1864.

22. MODEL. One gun on carriage. and two on slides, on the inside principle. Naval service.
Proposed by Mr. J. Edye. 1837.   1864.

23. MODEL. Gun and carriage. Naval service. 1864.

24. MODEL. Gun and carriage. Naval service. 1864.

25. MODEL. Gun and carriage, with one pair of trucks, as fitted to H.M.S. " DAPHNE," 18 guns. Built 1838. Naval service.   1864.

26. MODEL. Gun with carriage, fitted with lever to raise and lower the bed and quoin. Naval service. 1864.

27. MODEL. Carronade, on the inside principle, as fitted to H.M.S. " LIBERTY," 16 guns. Built. Naval service.
1864.

28. MODEL 32-pounder carronade, fitted on the inside principle, with slide shortened for quarter deck. Naval service.   1864.

29. PORT, with fittings for a carronade on the non-recoil principle. Naval service.   1864.

30. SHACKLE AND THIMBLE for gun. Proposed for Naval service.   1864.

31. Wood pattern SHACKLE for gun-breeching. Proposed for Naval service.   1864.

32. PROJECTILES ; made of " Atlas " toughened cast steel, in 1864. Broken and slotted to show the density and tough nature of the steel.
The Atlas Steel and Iron Works Co., Sheffield.
1864.
1. Projectile ; spherical shot, 8 inches in diameter.
2. Projectile; long shot, 12 × 7½ inches.
3. Projectile ; long shot, 16¾ × 10½ inches.
4. Projectile ; long shot, 13 × 8¼ inches, broken and slotted transversely.
The above four projectiles, made by the Atlas Steel and Iron Works Co., Sheffield, about 1860.

CLASS XII.

Models of Home Vessels.—Fishing and Pilot Boats—
Sailing and Steam Barges—Hoys and Lighters—
Canal Boats—River Steam Boats—Pleasure Yachts.

---

1. HALF BLOCK MODEL of a WHITBY five-man Fishing
Boat. Length, 57 ft.; breadth, 17 ft.; depth, 8 ft. 4 in.;
registered tonnage, 45 tons.
    Lent by Mr. T. Turnbull, A.I.N.A.   1869.

2. HALF BLOCK MODEL of a "COBLE" of the Yorkshire
coast. Each five-man fishing boat carries two cobles.
The flat after end allows them to be easily beached. When
under sail a rudder projecting 4 ft. below the stern is used.
    Lent by Mr. T. Turnbull, A.I.N.A.   1869.

3. HALF BLOCK MODEL of a fishing "MULE" of the
Yorkshire coast. Coble form forward; yawl form aft.
    Length, 33 ft. 9 in.; breadth, 10 ft.; depth, 4 ft. 9 in.
Scale, 1 in. to 1 ft.
    Lent by Mr. T. Turnbull, A.I.N.A., Whitby.   1871.

4. WHOLE MODEL, rigged, of a Thames sailing BARGE.
Built 1855. Length 70 ft.; breadth 16 ft.; depth 6 ft.
    Lent by Searle & Sons, Lambeth.   1865.

4a. WHOLE MODEL of a Thames Lighter or Barge, 1850.
For carrying grain, coal, and other merchandize. Scale of
model ½ inch to 1 foot.
    Presented by Messrs. Searle and Sons, Lambeth, 1851.
                                                          1877.
    Note.—This model of a Thames lighter is properly and
correctly built. The inside is left partly unplanked to show
the timbers. The outside is planked and finished. The plan
view shows the hold, flooring, bow and stern fittings, and
other detail.
    See Nos. 2, 23, 24, Class IX., pp. 83, 88, 89, and page 134.

5. WHOLE MODEL of the fore and aft schooner yacht
"KALAFISH." 60 tons burden. Designed and built by

owner Dr. J. Collis Browne, late Army Medical Staff, and belonging to Royal Cinque Ports Yacht Club, Dover.
Lent by Dr. J. Collis Browne.   1874.

Note.—The projection of the vessel's bow, or her beak, as it may be called, is built on the watertight compartment system. The object is to obtain more buoyancy forward for the yacht, and to render her a dry ship. Her dimensions are as follows :—Length, deck, 62 feet ; beak at bow, 12 feet ; total length over all, 74 feet ; beam, 16½ feet ; depth, 7½ feet ; draft, forward, 1 foot 6 inches ; aft, 5 feet 6 inches. Scale of model, ¾ inch to 1 foot.

6. WHOLE MODEL of the Woodside ferry paddle steam boat "CHESHIRE," employed between Birkenhead and Liverpool. Licensed to carry 1,620 passengers. Draught of water 6 ft. Designed by Mr. George Harrison, M.I.C.E.
The Millwall Iron Works Company.   1864.

7. WHOLE MODEL (on about ¼ inch scale) of the schooner yacht "AMERICA." Length 95 ft., beam 22 ft. Draft forward, 7 feet ; aft, 11 feet. Tons 210. Built 1851. Designed by Mr. Steers, New York. Rebuilt by Mr. Henry Pitcher at Northfleet.

Note.—The "AMERICA," yacht, was in America during the early part of the Civil war, 1860–1864, and sunk by the Federals. This is the famous yacht which came over from America in 1851 to challenge the yachts of England, and beat the "TITANIA" 4 minutes and 45 seconds in a run of 20 miles before the wind, and 45 minutes returning by the wind.

The advantage of the "AMERICA" may in some measure be attributed to her having cotton canvas instead of flax, and to the very superior manner in which her sails were cut, together with the fact that her tonnage was about double that of the "TITANIA."

Lent by Mr. John Scott Russell, F.R.S.   1868.

8. WHOLE MODEL of the iron paddle-wheel steamer "QUEEN." Built and fitted with engines by J. and G. Rennie, 1842. Length 160 ft., depth 9 ft. Speed between 17 and 18 miles per hour, which exceeded that of any vessel on the Thames.
Lent by Messrs. J. and G. Rennie, Engineers,
Holland Street, Blackfriars.   1876

9. WHOLE MODEL of a Yarmouth Trawling SMACK. Rigged. Without the trawl net.
Lent by Mr. John Bracey, Yarmouth.   1876.

10. HALF MODEL the "MARY TAYLOR," New York pilot boat. Built in New York, by George Steers an Englishman, about 1850.

He afterwards built the celebrated "AMERICA" yacht. He told the exhibitor in New York, in September 1854, that he considered the "MARY TAYLOR" the faster vessel of the two, particularly in rough water.
Lent by Mr. Henry Liggins, 3, Ladbroke Square, Bayswater.   1876.

11. HALF BLOCK MODEL of small Screw Steamer " MAB," the fastest on the Neva. Built in 1874, of brass, by George Baird, C.E., St. Petersburgh.

Length	- - -	- 48 ft.
Breadth	- - -	- 6 ft. 6 in.
Depth at side -	- -	- 3 „ 6 „
Draught	- -	- 1 „ 7 „
„ over screw	- -	- 2 „ 9 „
Speed	- - -	- 19 miles.
Diameter of high pressure cylinder	-	7 ins.
„ low „		- 11 „
Stroke	- -	- 8 „
Working pressure	- -	- 120 lbs.
Revolutions per minute	-	- 600

Lent by Mr. George Baird, C.E., St. Petersburgh.
1876.

12. Drawing of the Paddle Steamer " ELIZABETH," built by Charles Baird in 1815, and run on the river Neva St. Petersburgh.
Lent by Mr. George Baird, C.E., St. Petersburgh,
1876.

Note.—She was constructed out of a barge, and the chimney was of brick. The floats of the paddle-wheels were kept in a vertical position by means of shafts and mitre wheels. Scale of drawing ¼ inch to the foot.

13. Drawing of Paddle-wheel Steamer, built by Charles Baird in 1817. To carry passengers between Petersburg and Cronstadt. Showing end view, longitudinal view, plan, and longitudinal section.
Lent by Mr. George Baird, C.E., St. Petersburgh.
1876.

Note.—References to drawing.

A. Steam engine.
B. Boiler.
C. C. Crank shafts on either side, with fly-wheel.
D. D. Toothed wheels driving paddle-wheel.
E. E. Paddle-wheels with floats revolving 50 turns per minute, by which the vessel is propelled.
F. Funnel leading from furnace serving in place of a mast.
G. G. Fore and aft cabins.
H. H. Side decks, to protect the wheels from the blows of the waves.
I. I. Paddle-boxes.
K. L. Staircase and rudder.
Scale of drawing, ¼″ to 1 foot.

14. WHOLE MODEL of a Harbour Steam Dredging Machine; built of iron, propelled by twin screws, and showing the chief fittings and improvements carried out by the builders Thomas Wingate and Company.

Lent by Messrs. Thomas Wingate and Company,
Engineers and Shipbuilders, Whiteinch, Glasgow.
1877.

Note.—This model is a working model, so far as the dredging machinery is concerned; being fitted with copper boiler and working engine. It also shows the upper deck arrangements of this kind of vessel which is employed for the heaviest sort of work in harbour dredging.

CLASS XIII.

Foreign Craft and Vessels of all kinds.

1. WHOLE MODEL, rigged, of the Viceroy of Egypt's Yacht, for the river Nile.
Presented by the Egyptian Commissioner for the Paris
    Exhibition of 1867.   1868.

2. WHOLE MODEL of the American river side-wheel steamer "EMPIRE;" of the New York and Albany line of steamers running on the river Hudson.
Presented by Mr. D. Lapraike.   1868.

    Note.—This model shows particularly the ship's construction, the disposition of the passenger accommodation, and the emplacement of the boilers, steering wheel house, &c.

3. MODEL, rigged, of a Ceylon Boat.   Length 14 in., breadth 1 inch.   Outrigger, 7½ inches over all.
Presented by Mr. T. D. E. Gibson.   1865.

4. MODEL, rigged, of a Cingalese outrigger Canoe. Length 2 ft. 2 inch, breadth 1¼ inch.   Over all, 10 inches, outrigger.
Lent by Mr. Thos. F. Dodd.   1868.

5. WHOLE MODELS. Three masted Chinese Junk. Six Chinese boats.

    Length of the junk, 21 in., breadth 5½ in.
    Length of the boats, 20 in., breadth 4 in.

,,	,,	17½ ,,	,,	3½ ,,	
,,	,,	14 ,,	,,	4 ,,	
,,	,,	10 ,,	,,	2¼ ,,	
,,	,,	9 ,,	,,	3 ,,	
,,	,,	4½ ,,	,,	1½ ,,	

Presented by Mr. J. Pybus.   1868.

6. WHOLE MODEL of a three-masted Chinese Junk: rigged.   Length 4 ft. 2 in., breadth 11 in., depth 7 in. The model shows upper deck fittings, hatchways, cooking galley, cabins, &c.
Presented by Mr. W. T. Lay.   1870.

7. MODEL of an Ancient Maltese Galley, supposed to have belonged to one of the Grand Masters of the Knights of Malta, together with a small painting containing a representation of the galley, and probably of contemporary date

with it.   Length of model, 6 ft. 2 in., breadth 14½ in.,
depth 6 in.
>   Lent by Mr. W. Ladd, late Master Shipwright, Dept-
>   ford Dockyard.   1864.

8. WHOLE MODEL of a Bombay pleasure Boat or
yacht, full rigged. Two-masted boat, with latteen sails,
running gear, deck fittings, &c.   Length of model 3 ft.
7 in., beam 7¼ in., extreme depth 7 in. Scale about 1 in.
to 1 ft.
>   Presented by H.R.H. the Duke of Edinburgh.   1871.

9. MODEL of a Fiji or Feejee double Sailing Canoe.
Rigged with mast and sails, complete. Made by natives of
the Fiji or Feejee islands.   Length of major canoe 3 ft.
3 in. ; minor canoe 2 feet 11 in.   Extreme breadth 18½ in.
>   Presented by Sir D. Cooper, F.R.G.S.   1872.

10. MODEL of the Nile dakabeah "MARIANNE."   Constructed by Rev. A. J. Foster.   Scale ¼ in. to 1 ft.
>   Lent by Rev. A. J. Foster.   1873.

11. TREE CANOE.   From the Hudson's Bay Territory.
Length 19 feet, breadth 2 ft. 8½ in.
>   Presented by the Hudson's Bay Company.   1870.

12. ESQUIMAUX CANOE.   From the Hudson's Bay
Territory.   Length 20 ft., breadth 1 ft. 6 in.
>   Presented by the Hudson's Bay Company.   1870.

13. BIRCH BARK CANOE.   From the Hudson's Bay
Territory.   Length 19 ft., breadth 2 ft. 10½ in.
>   Presented by the Hudson's Bay Company.   1870.
>   *Also* nine paddles belonging to above three canoes,
>   from Hudson's Bay Territory.
>   Presented by the Hudson's Bay Company.   1870.

14. MODEL, rigged, of a Cingalese outrigger Canoe.
Length extreme, 3 feet 4½ inches ; beam, ¼ inch ; length of
outrigger, 2 feet 2 inches extreme ; extreme breadth over
all, 15 inches.
>   Presented by Mr. W. R. Page, Putney.   1874.

CLASS XIV.

Lighthouses. Harbour and Coast Lights. Light Ships, &c. Mark Buoys.

---

1. WHOLE MODEL. The Light Ship stationed on the Goodwin Sands; with lanterns, and all fitments complete, for day and night service. Scale ½ inch to 1 foot.

Note.—The following are the principal dimensions of the Goodwin Sands Lightship :—

Length 96 ft., breadth 21 ft., depth 10 ft. 8 in. Tons 195.
Height of main globe from water line, 58 ft.
Weight of mushroom (anchor), 42 cwt.
Size of chain cable 1½ in., Length of cable 210 fathoms.
The port side of the vessel shows the ship built complete.
Starboard side shows the timbers, waling, &c.

Lent by the Corporation of the Trinity House. 1865.

2. MODEL IN WOOD of the existing Eddystone Lighthouse, made by George Knott, for many years lightkeeper on the rock.

Lent by the Corporation of the Trinity House. 1866.

Note.—The Eddystone Rocks, so named from the great variety of sets of tides and currents which surround them, are situated about 14 miles S.S.W. of the port of Plymouth, the sea being fully 30 fathoms in depth. A lighthouse was constructed on these rocks by Winstanley in 1696, and destroyed by a storm in 1703. A second was built by Rudyerd in 1709, and was totally consumed by fire in 1755. The present lighthouse was commenced in 1755–56, and completed in 1759, by John Smeaton, F.R.S., civil engineer, Born 1724, died 1792.

3. MODEL of the Lighthouse on the Eddystone Rock, off the coast of Cornwall, 1757–1759.

Lent by the Corporation of Trinity House. 1874.

Note.—This Model represents the existing stone lighthouse built on the Eddystone Rock by John Smeaton, engineer. It was begun in 1756–7 and finished 1759.

The light (fixed) was first shown on October 21, 1759.

It has been found necessary this year (1877) to consider the taking down and rebuilding, on another rock anew, the Eddystone Lighthouse ; owing to the undermining action of the sea upon the rock on which the present light stands.

4. MODEL of the Gunfleet Lighthouse. Iron. Built on Mitchell's patent screw piles, of which a model is shown. The piles screw 40 ft. into the sand and have screws 4 ft. in diameter. James Walker, engineer.

Lent by the Corporation of the Trinity House.   1874.

5. MODEL of the Lighthouse on the Needles Rocks, Isle of Wight. Built 1857–1858. Light shown January 1, 1859. J. Walker, engineer, T. Ormiston, executive.

Lent by the Corporation of the Trinity House.   1874.

6. MODEL of the Lighthouse on the Great Basses Rocks, Ceylon. Begun 1870, finished 1872. Shows a revolving red light, giving flashes at 45 seconds interval, at 110 ft. above high water. Light was first shown March 15, 1873.

Lent by the Corporation of the Trinity House.   1874.

Note.—This lighthouse was built from designs by James N. Douglas, M.I.C.E., under the superintendence of William Douglas, M.I.C.E. The tower is of Scotch granite (Dalbeattie), each stone of which was dressed, fitted, and marked in this country

7. MODEL of the Lighthouse on the Wolf Rock, coast of Cornwall. Begun 1864, finished 1869. Shows a fixed red light at 119 ft. above high water. Light first shown January 1, 1871. J. N. Douglas, engineer.

Lent by the Corporation of the Trinity House.   1874.

8. MODEL of the Old Lighthouse on the Smalls Rocks, about 17 miles off the coast of Pembrokeshire. Erected 1776 ; replaced in 1861 by a stone lighthouse. The model is made out of one of the oak piles of the original lighthouse.

The executors of the late Captain Pickering Clarke, R.N.   1862.

9. HARBOUR LIGHT. Chance's dioptric lens of the fourth order for fixed light.

Lent by Messrs. Chance Brothers & Co., glass works, Birmingham.   1874.

10. BABBAGE'S apparatus for an Occulting Light in lighthouses.

Lent by Major-General Babbage.   1876.

Note.—This piece of mechanism was designed in 1850 by the late Mr. C. Babbage (*b.* 1791—*d.* 1871), with a view of rendering lighthouses distinguishable from one another at sea by night, by means of a given number of flashes of light occulting in a preconcerted order. The number of consecutive flashes counted and their duration would form a means of determining the exact lighthouse seen, and thus mariners would be able to fix accurately the position of their ship when opposite any line of the coast. Mr. Babbage also invented the celebrated calculating machine known by his name, now exhibited in the Educational Division of the Museum.

11. SERIES OF MODELS, illustrating Mark Buoys, used by the Trinity House Corporation round the British coast.

Lent by the Corporation of the Trinity House.   1874.

Note.—The Models are on a scale about 1 in. to 1 ft., and represent iron and wooden buoys with their anchorage. The following are the Mark Buoys represented by the models :—

A Bell Buoy, 8 ft.
Egg-bottom Buoy, 12 ft.
Hollow Bottom Buoy, Herbert's pattern.
Reversed Can, 8 ft.
Convex Buoy, wood, 8 ft.
9 ft. Can, wood.
8 ft. Can, wood.
Wreck Buoy, wood.
17 ft. Can.
7 ft. Can, wood.

12. PHOTOGRAPHS illustrating Dioptric Apparatus for Lighthouses, by Chance, Brothers, & Co., Glass works, Birmingham.

Lent   1875.

12*a.* First Order Revolving Light, eight sides.   For the Longstone, Fern Islands, 1873.

12*b.* First Order Revolving Light, with alternate red and white flashes of equal intensity ; 9 sides. For Hartland Point, Devon, 1873. Views showing great lens (69° 28') for the red flash.

12*c.* First Order Revolving Light, with alternate red and white flashes of equal intensity ; 9 sides. For Hartland Point, Devon, 1873. Views showing red shades (69° 28') for the red flash.

12*d.* First Order Revolving Light, with 6 sides (60° each) with Subsidiary Apparatus (fifth order Holophate and totally reflecting prisms) by which a fixed light is exhibited at a lower level. For Start Point, Devon, 1873.

12*e.* Fourth Order Condensing Light, with fixed apparatus, Holophote, and Vertical Prisms. For Cowan, Cowan Point, Queensland, 1874.

12*f*. Fourth Order Condensing Light, with fixed apparatus, Holophotes and Vertical Prisms. For Cowan, Cowan Point, Queensland, 1874.

12*g*. First Order Revolving Light, alternate red and white flashes of equal intensity. For the Wolf Rock, coast of Cornwall. Front view of red shades, 1869.

12*h*. First Order Revolving Light, alternate red and white flashes of equal intensity. For the Wolf Rock, coast of Cornwall. View showing red shades half opened, 1869.

12*i*. Revolving Light (of the Second and Third Order) for the Electric Spark. For Souter Point, coast of Northumberland. View showing main apparatus and subsidiary apparatus for the lower light, 1870.

12*j*. First Order Revolving Light, eight sides. For Boompjes, Java, 1870.

12*k*. Fourth Order Revolving Light. For the Government of Brazil, 1871.

12*l*. Third Order Fixed Light, for the Electric Spark. For South Foreland High Lighthouse. Front view, 1871.

12*m*. Third Order Fixed Light for the Electric Spark. For South Foreland High Lighthouse. Back view showing intensifying agents, 1871.

12*n*. Second Order Light, fifteen sides; exhibiting Triple Flashes in rapid succession in groups, at intervals of half-a-minute, with new Clockwork and Centrifugal Governor. For Mexico, 1875.

12*o*. Type of a First Order, Fixed Light. As made for the Trinity House of London. View with figures to show scale.

12*p*. First Order Fixed Light, with Vertical Condensing Prisms. For Bidstone Lighthouse, near Birkenhead. For Mersey Docks and Harbour Board, 1872.

12*q*. Fifth Order Fixed Light, with Vertical Condensing Prisms and Holophote. For the Port of Dublin, 1872.

12*r*. Second Order Revolving Light, showing clockwork and lamp. For the Gun-Cay Lighthouse, Bahamas, 1872.

NOTE upon Lenses and Apparatus for Lighthouses.

EXTRACTED from Information given on this subject by the LIGHTHOUSE SERVICE of FRANCE, 1876.

First essay.—Echeloned lens, polygonal form. Invented by A. Fresnel, and constructed under his direction in 1819.

First echeloned lens, polygonal form, for flashing lights of the first class. Invented by A. Fresnel, and constructed in 1820.

First echeloned lens, annular form, for flashing lights of the first class. Invented by A. Fresnel, and proceeding from the lenticular apparatus fixed on the tower of Cordouan in 1821.

When Fresnel conceived the idea of substituting in lighthouses for metallic reflectors large glass lenses, he thought of composing these lenses of several pieces, and of calculating the curves of these different pieces so as to rectify their spherical divergence. He demonstrated his plan before the Lighthouse Committee, in August 1819, three months only after his appointment on the Committee, and on the 19th of October following he was granted the sum of 500 fr. for constructing a trial lens. He consulted the optician Soleil, who seconded him with much good will, but who could only put at his disposal the limited appliances then in use. Glass was at this time worked still by hand, and shaped only into plane or spherical forms. Fresnel admitted that the lens should be flat on one side ; that the different gradients, instead of forming circular rings, should be defined by polygons and divided into a certain number of pieces, each of which should receive on its echeloned side a spherical surface properly calculated. Another difficulty arose from the glass factories being unable to supply in sufficient size pieces of crown glass free from bubbles and striæ ; but Fresnel discovered the way of re-smelting glass without altering its transparency.

He first constructed a trial lens of 35 centimetres diameter. It was given by Soleil to the Academy of Sciences, and deposited at the " Conservatoire des Arts et Métiers." It is composed of 21 pieces, glued together, and fixed upon a flat pane which serves as a support.

Emboldened by this first success, Fresnel proposed to the Lighthouse Committee, at their sitting of 31st December 1820, to order the construction of a lenticular revolving light apparatus for the Cordouan lighthouse. The principal part of this apparatus was to include eight square lenses of 76 centimetres, forming together an octagonal prism inscribed within a cylinder of 2m. diameter. This proposal was adopted, and Mr. Soleil undertook the construction of these eight polygonal echeloned lenses. It was composed of 100 pieces of glass, glued together, and the flat pane, which in the trial lens serves as a support, has been done away with. One of these new lenses was first tried in public on 13th April 1821. It was placed on the top of the Observatory buildings, together with two large reflectors, one by Lenoir, the other by Bordier-Marcet. The Lighthouse Committee, of which Mr.

Becquey, director-general of the "Ponts et Chaussées," was chairman, went to the summit of Montmartre to judge of the effect. The result confirmed the inventor's previsions, and every one allowed the superiority of the lens over the reflectors. Meanwhile, Fresnel had already thought of improving these first essays. He had invented a machine for constructing circular rings, and M. Soleil was instructed to make eight large lenses constructed on annular principles. He soon finished some of them, and in September 1821 the Lighthouse Committee determined to try their effect at long distances. Fresnal had fitted up on the top of the "Arc de l'Etoile" a revolving apparatus upon which were fixed two of these annular lenses, four polygonal lenses previously constructed, and four semi-polygonal lenses. At the focus, a four-wicked lamp was burning. The committee then went to Chateney, a village situated N.N.E. of Paris, 24½ kilometres distance from the "Arc de l'Etoile." The experiment took place during the night of 7/8 September 1821, and the results were adjudged as very satisfactory. The eight annular lenses that had just been constructed form part of the first flashing-light apparatus of the 1st class that Fresnel himself fixed on the watch-tower of Cordouan, and which has lighted the entrance to the Gironde for more than 30 years.

If an idea is to be formed of the progress made in the science of lenticular lighthouses from its origin to later times, the three lenses before mentioned should be compared with the lenses of modern construction.

Fixed Light Apparatus.

First fixed light apparatus of 0·50^m diameter. Invented by A. Fresnel, and constructed in 1824.

Fresnel, after his appointment to the Lighthouse Committee of 1819, first gave his attention to flashing lights; meanwhile, he had thought about obtaining fixed lights, and in the first design of the lenticular lighthouse that he submitted to the committee on 31st October 1820, he indicated, as a solution, the use of cylindrical lenses; but the lighthouse Committee had thrown aside the fixed light system as possessing less reverberating power that revolving lights, and as being liable to be mistaken for the incidental lights of the coasts. The committee altered this decision later, and Fresnel then invented the system of fixed light apparatus (0·50^m diameter); in this apparatus the lenticular drum, which should be cylindrical, so as to give an uniform subdivision of light, shows a polygonal form of 16 fasces, because no lathe was then known for making cylindrical pieces. The upper part is made up of two lenticular zones in the shape of a 16-panel cupola, every element of which is coupled with a plane mirror. The lenses unite in parallel fasces the rays emitted by the light, and the mirrors reflect them in the direction of the horizon.

A similar system, but having one lenticular zone only, is fitted at the lower part. The lamp has two wicks, and stands upon a plate raised or lowered by a jack between three leaders. With the polygonal form that had to be adopted, there were 16 directly receiving more light than the intermediate parts, but Fresnel, while constructing the instrument, discovered the means of greatly lessening this inequality, by alternating the shining directions of the lenticular cylinders with those of the two other parts. This first trial of a fixed light apparatus was demonstrated by Fresnel before the Acadamy of Sciences of Paris, at their sittings of 3rd May 1824. It was then inaugurated on the 1st February 1825 in the port of Dunkirk.

Catadioptric Rings.

First apparatus containing catadioptric rings, as well for fixed as for flashing lights. Invented by A. Fresnel, for lighting the St. Martin Canal, and constructed in 1825.

Annular lens, composed of dioptric and catadioptric elements, similar to those of apparatus No. 5, and constructed at the same date.

Models in wood of a similar apparatus, but on a larger scale. Study of A. Fresnel in 1825.

The last invention of A. Fresnel, that of the catadioptric rings, resulted from a request for information addressed to him by the Prefect of the Seine in 1825. It was a question of applying to lighting the quays of the St. Martin's Canal more powerful lamps than those used commonly in the city of Paris. This problem, to which Fresnel's attention was called, was the same as that of the port-lights apparatus, of which he had postponed the study because the sidereal reflectors of Bordier-Marcet were sufficient to supply the wants of the service.

The principal part of these small apparatus, that is, the lenticular cylinder, offered no theoretical difficulty. It was to proceed out of an echeloned section turning around the vertical axis; the only thing was to construct it in circular shape, because the polygonal shape would have been impossible for rings of 20 to 25 centimetres diameter. The question was not so easily solved as regards the accessory parts intended to utilise the luminous rays passing outside the cylinder, because the reflectors used in the other classes had to be reduced to very small dimensions. It was then that Fresnel thought of the phenomenon known in optics under the name of "total reflection," and imagined to substitute for the common reflectors, glass rings, within which the luminous rays should be reflected without appreciable loss.

Fresnel's first conception for these circular rings was to direct the fasces through which the luminous rays pass perpendicularly to these rays, so as not to alter their direction; the reflecting surface would then have preserved the shape of the mirrors to be replaced, but hence resulted inconvenience, and a too great weight of glass. Fresnel found out that an inclined direction upon the rays could be given to these in and out going fasces, and these inclinations be combined, as well as the shape of the reflecting surface, so as to force the rays to emerge horizontally. The transverse section of the rings then became triangular instead of showing four sides, and the dimensions lessened.

In the apparatus to which Fresnel first applied this invention the diameter is reduced to $0·20^m$; the cylinder is generated by an echeloped section composed of three elements and fills up a half circumference. The rays passing above this cylinder are gathered by four total-reflection rings, and this is effected by turning around the vertical point of the focus, the section of the catadioptric triangles just spoken off. Thus is obtained a fixed light apparatus, lighting up half the horizon. The lamps of the St. Martin's Canal having to be erected at 70 metres distance, it became necessary to give them a greater lateral than frontal intenseness. Fresnel succeeded in this by placing on each side a half annular dioptric lens, generated by the rotation of the section of the cylinder around an horizontal axis, parallel with the longitudinal direction of the quay, but he had moreover the happy idea of making the section of catadioptric triangles to revolve around this axis so as to form an annular lens, collecting around the focus an angle of great amplitude, and comprising at the same time dioptric and catadioptric rings.

The manufacture of these different circular rings offered serious difficulty, and Fresnel was obliged to set up a factory.

A first apparatus was completed in 1826, and submitted to the Lighthouse Committee towards the end of December. Four of these new lamps were finished at the beginning of 1827, but they could not be tried until after the inventor's death.

This study shows how Fresnel came to invent not only the section of catadioptric rings, and the use of these rings in fixed light apparatus, but also their application to annular lenses for flashing lights or for fixed lights. By uniting the pieces of dioptric elements and of catadioptric rings manufactured in Fresnel's time for the apparatus of the St. Martin's Canal, the annular lens was formed, and it may be considered as the type of all the annular lenses used in the lighthouses of different orders.

The model in wood represents an apparatus similar to the preceding, but having a diameter of $0·25^m$ instead of $0·20^m$. It is a study of Fresnel's which he did not carry out.

Lighthouse Lamp Burners.

One of the first burners, with four concentric wicks, was constructed in 1819–20 after experiments made by Arago and Fresnel.

A burner, with two wicks and outer wrapper for directing the draught, was constructed by Henry Lepaute in 1845.

A burner, with five wicks, of graduated shape, for mineral oil, with the last improvements adopted in the lighthouses of France, 1876.

When Fresnel undertook the improvement of lighthouses, he had to solve not only the problem of construction of the lenses, but also that of lamps with several wicks. The chemist Guyton-Morvau had already studied the question. In a paper read by him at the Institute in 1797, he stated that he had constructed 10 years before a lamp on the argand principle, with three concentric circular wicks, each having an inner and an outer draught. He acquired great intenseness, but the solderings of the burner were destroyed by the heat.   About 1800 the watchmaker Carcel invented the lamp that bears his name, and in which the oil at the bottom is forced up by a pump towards the burner above which it overflows.   This invention was to lead towards solving the problem of lamps with many wicks.   Consequently, when Arago and Fresnel began, in 1819, their experiments with lamps, they forced up the burner oil in superabundance so as to refresh it, and thus avoid the inconvenience met with by Guyton-Morvau. The first trial took place in September 1819 with two-wicked and three-wicked burners, constructed after Fresnel's designs.   After several hesitations, respecting chiefly the width to be adopted for the draught between the wicks, they succeeded in constructing a a four-wicked burner that gave good results.   It was tried 12th May 1820, in presence of the Lighthouse Committee.

The two-wick burner was constructed by Henry Lepaute in 1845 for the lighthouse of Schevening in Holland.   It has an outer cylinder for dividing the draught generated between the blast and the burner, and throwing back a part of it upon the light.   It is the first application of this cylinder which exists in all modern burners.

The five-wick burner is now constructed for all the French lighthouses and for burning mineral oils.   It contains an appendage through which the oil must pass before reaching the upper part of the burner.   This apparatus, of which the arrangements were invented by M. Dénéchaux, acting engineer in ordinary at the lighthouse depôt, is intended to secure a continuous level, and comprises three tubes, juxtaposed, and open on the upper part at the proper height ; the central tube springs from the small reservoir which forms the basis of the burner, and in which the oil is forced by the machinery of the lamp ; this oil, having no other exit, rises in the tube, and, arriving at the top, flows into the second tube, which carries it into the annular spaces containing the wicks ; these it fills while keeping the same level as in the lateral appendage.   As the quantity of oil forced up by the lamp is greater than the consumption, the excess comes down into the large reservoir of the lamp by flowing into the third tube over a fall rather higher than that cleared by the oil in reaching the burner.   A horizontal disk of 30 millimetres diameter rises, at the height of 21 millimetres, above the central draught tube, and an outer cylinder divides in two the draught created between the burner and the glass.   It is upon this outer cylinder that the glass-holder stands.   In this burner the empty spaces between the wicks, intended for air passages, are $5\frac{1}{2}$ millimeters wide, while the spaces that contain the wicks are only $4\frac{1}{2}$ millimetres.   In the burners constructed up to the present time, both widths are of 5 millimetres ; this new arrangement seems to give better results. The burner has besides, on its upper part, a graduated shape, so that each wick is placed about two millimeters below the one which precedes it towards the centre.   This arrangement, as yet adopted only for the Pilier lighthouse, has been found necessary since the burners, in each order of lighthouses, have had one burner added to them, and therefore wider.   Its object is to lower the edge of the burner, in reference to the centre of the light, so as to reduce as much as possible the portion of light obscured by this edge in the lower part of the lenses.

Modern Lighthouse Apparatus.

Great annular lens, of the first order, $1 \cdot 10^m$ in diameter, Messrs. Barbier and Fenestre, constructors, 1867. This lens was constructed by Messrs. Barbier and Fenestre as a specimen of high class workmanship. Each ring is one single piece; the joints which divide the rings are inclined according to the direction of the ray refracted. The lens mounted on a pedestal revolves around a horizontal axis.

Lenticular panel, dioptric and catadioptric, for flashing lights of the second class, planned by the head engineer, Allard, and constructed by Mr. Henry Lepaute, 1876.

It forms part of an apparatus intended for the Pilier lighthouse, situated at the mouth of the Loire, and of which the tower has just been rebuilt. The character given to it in 1829 has been preserved; it is a fixed light varied by flashes every four minutes. To produce this character a fixed light apparatus has been adopted, of which two sectors of $\frac{1}{4}$th horison, opposed to one another, are replaced by perfect annular lenses; it revolves at the rate of one turn in eight minutes. In order that the two kinds of lenses may be adjusted upon the edges, and have a common pinion-jack, the focal distance, which is $0 \cdot 700^m$ for the fixed lenses, has been reduced to $0 \cdot 647^m$ for the annular lenses. The focal lamp has five concentric wicks, instead of four, as usual in lamps of the second class, because the light, being coloured red in certain directions, it was thought necessary to increase its intenseness.

The panel shows several novel arrangements, some of which are now for the first time applied.

1st. In the central or dioptric parts of the section, the joints that divide the elements, and therefore the lower sides of these elements, instead of being horizontal, are inclined according to the direction of the ray refracted. This system has several advantages: it does away with a triangular part of glass which is useless, and thus lessens the weight of the apparatus; it reduces in a large proportion the loss of light caused by horizontal joints; it makes less harsh and consequently less fragile, the outer angles of the elements, and besides diminishes their projection, thus enabling the dioptric lens to acquire a greater height.

2nd. The central lens (or dioptric) comprehends a vertical angle of 76 degrees, whereas, in the old sections, this angle was of about 60 degress only; its elevation is thus increased from $0 \cdot 85^m$ to $1 \cdot 10^m$. This advantage is thus obtained, that the luminous rays meet the last dioptric element at the same angle as the first catadioptric ring, and suffer no more loss of reflection upon the one than upon the other.

3rd. The section commonly used in apparatus of the second class had been calculated for a three-wick lamp burner of $0 \cdot 074^m$ diameter. With a five-wick burner of $1 \cdot 110^m$ diameter, the inferior elements of the dioptric lens and the lower catadioptric rings, constructed after this old section, emit rays that are no longer in the proper direction, because the portion of light which the base of the burner leaves visible becomes perceptibly nearer to the lens than in the case of a three-wick burner. To lessen this defect, a graduated shape was given to the burner, by placing each wick 0.002^m below the one preceding it on the side of the centre. This arrangement reduces neither the regularity nor the intensity of the light, and the part of the light, visible from each of the lower lenticular elements, becomes somewhat increased. Moreover, these lower elements have been calculated by determining for each of them a particular focus taken on the brightest line of the apparent part of the light, instead of on the axis itself of the lamp.

4th. The central lens and the lower rings are included in the same frame, the upper rings are set in a second frame, separated from the first by a metal cross-beam. In the annular lenses, this cross-beam takes the shape of the arc of a circle having like the rings, its centre on the optical axis; the result is that the rings remain intact, instead of having to be cut.

5th. The lamp, used at the focus of the lens, shows special arrangements due to M. Dénéchaux.

The lamp with five wicks for burning mineral oil has an intenseness of 36 carcel burners, the fixed light apparatus produces an intenseness of 640 burners, and the annular lenses produce an effulgence of more than 5,000 burners.

Apparatus for electric revolving light, constructed by Messrs. Sautter, Limonnier, & Co., 1876.

This instrument is intended to produce, by electric light, a light revolving at intervals of 30 seconds. It includes a fixed light apparatus 0.50^m diameter, lighting the three-fourths of the horizon, around which revolves, in eight minutes, a drum 0.62^m diameter, and composed of 16 vertical, lenticular elements.

In the section of the fixed light apparatus the central dioptric part fills vertically an angle of 76 degrees, which is greater than in the old sections. This arrangement is adopted in order that the luminous ray may meet the last dioptric element at the same angle as the first catadioptric ring, and should suffer no more loss by reflection upon the one than upon the other. The apparatus designed for an elevated position, the section of the several parts, except that of the two lowest catadioptric rings, has been calculated so as to throw the focal line of the emergent rays, 30 minutes below the horizontal line ; in the calculation of the two lowest rings, this angle is increased by three degrees for the last but one, and by five degrees for the last, so that the lighthouse may remain visible at a short distance, that is, by a navigator placed below the divergent cone emitted by the rest of the apparatus.

The 16 vertical lenses are contiguous, and are each composed of a single element, about 0.12 wide, the curve of which has been calculated so as to give with the electric light an horizontal divergence of three degrees seven minutes. The duration of a flash is, accordingly, of about five seconds, and the interval between the end of a flash and the beginning of the following one is 25 seconds.

The maximum intenseness of the flash rises to about 60,000

burners, assuming at the focus an electric light of 200-burner power.

The light is produced in this apparatus, as in the lighthouses established on the coasts of France, by means of a Serrin regulator and an electrical machine of the Compagnie l'Alliance.

Experiments have been made with the Serrin regulator at the lighthouse dépôt since the year 1860. A model on a large scale has been constructed especially for the lighthouse service, and has always given good results.

The electro-magnetic machine has been, and is well known, designed by MM. Nollet and Joseph Van Walderen, in accordance with the same principle as the scientific apparatus of Pixii and Clarke. It produces alternate currents, and, as it was in the first instance destined for the decomposition of water or for electro metallurgy, it was provided with a commutator for bringing the currents into one constant direction. When the question was raised of applying it to the production of light, M. Van Malderen, who had then become the mechanical engineer to the Compagnie l'Alliance, conceived the idea of suppressing the commutator, which is difficult to maintain and has the effect of more or less weakening the current. The luminous intensity was found to be appreciably augmented, and the fact was soon acknowledged that alternate currents are, *cæteris paribus*, more favourable regulators than those in a constant direction. The machines of the Compagnie l'Alliance had originally six discs; these were reduced to four when the improvements into the coils and the magnets permitted of a greater intensity being obtained with these smaller machines than with the former. In the case of lighthouses, where there cannot be too great intensity, the number of six discs has been preserved.

The central dépôt in Paris has retained, since 1860, the first specimen constructed by M. Van Malderen of this machine, with the currents not brought into one constant direction. It has six discs, and carries 56 magnets ; it is 1·63 metre high, and 1·43 metre in diameter ; it gives less light than the present machines, but it works very well still, and serves for the experiments that are made at the dépôt.

The first machine of the Compagnie l'Alliance may be regarded as the starting point of all the attempts which have since been made of economically transforming power into electricity, and consequently into light.

The researches by Fresnel, described in this notice of lighthouse apparatus, may be said to be the foundation of all present systems for this branch of scientific construction.

A. J. Fresnel was born at Broglie in France in 1788, and died in 1827 near Paris. His discoveries and researches were especially in the diffraction and polarization of light.

*** The objects referred to in the foregoing account of Fresnel's researches are preserved in Paris by the Lighthouse Service of France.

CLASS XV.

Paintings, Drawings, Photographs, of Ships, and of Subjects in connexion with them.

OIL AND WATER COLOUR PAINTINGS.

1. STERN VIEW of H.M.S. "ROYAL GEORGE," 1st rate, 100 guns, length 178 ft. 0 in., breadth 51 ft. 9½ in., depth 21 ft. 6 in., tonnage 2,041.   Laid down at Woolwich Yard in 1746, launched in 1756, overset 29th August 1782, "she being heeled to come at the pipe that leads to the well."
The complement of men was 850.
Drawn by Josh. Williams, painted by Josh. Marshall, 1774.
Presented by Her Majesty.   1864.

2. BOW VIEW of H.M.S. "ROYAL GEORGE" (same ship as the preceding).
Drawn by J. Binmer, painted by Josh. Marshall, 1774.
Presented by Her Majesty.   1864.

3. STERN VIEW of H.M.S. "VICTORY," 1st rate, 100 guns, length 174 ft. 9 in., breadth 50 ft. 6 in., depth 20 ft. 6 in., tonnage 1,921.   Built at Portsmouth Yard in 1737.   Lost in the English Channel in the night between the 4th and 5th October 1744, when Admiral Balchin and the crew of upwards of 1,000 men perished.
Drawn by Josh. Williams, painted by Josh. Marshall, 1744.
Presented by Her Majesty.   1864.

4. BOW VIEW of H.M.S. "VICTORY," (same ship as the preceding).
Drawn by J. Binmer, painted by Josh. Marshall, 1774.
Presented by Her Majesty.   1864.

5. STERN VIEW of H.M.S. "BARFLEUR," 2nd rate, 90 guns, length 177 ft. 8 in., breadth 50 ft. 5 in., depth 21 ft., tonnage 750.   Laid down at Chatham Yard in 1762, launched in 1768, broken up in 1819.
The complement of men was 750.
Drawn by Josh. Williams, painted by Josh. Marshall, 1774.
Presented by Her Majesty.   1864.

6. Bow VIEW of H.M.S. "BARFLEUR" (same ship as the preceding).
Drawn by J. Binmer, painted by Josh. Marshall, 1774.
Presented by Her Majesty.   1864.

7. STERN VIEW of H.M.S. "ROYAL OAK," 3rd rate, 74 guns, length 168 ft. 6 in., breadth 46 ft. 9 in., depth 20 ft., tonnage 1,606. Laid down at Devonport Yard in 1766, launched in 1769, broken up in 1815.
The complement of men was 650.
Drawn by Josh. Williams, painted by Josh. Marshall, 1774.
Presented by Her Majesty.   1864.

8. Bow VIEW of H.M.S. "ROYAL OAK" (same ship as the preceding).
Drawn by J. Binmer, painted by Josh. Marshall, 1774.
Presented by Her Majesty.   1864.

9. STERN VIEW of H.M.S. "INTREPID," 3rd rate, 64 guns, length 159 feet. 6 in., breadth 44 ft. 5 in., depth 19 ft., tonnage 1,374. Laid down at Woolwich Yard in 1767, launched in 1770, sold in 1828.
The complement of men was 500.
Drawn by Josh. Williams, painted by Josh. Marshall, 1774.
Presented by Her Majesty.   1864.

10. Bow VIEW of H.M.S. "INTREPID" (same ship as the preceding).
Drawn by J. Binmer, painted by Josh Marshall, 1774.
Presented by Her Majesty.   1864.

11. STERN VIEW of H.M.S. "PORTLAND," 4th rate, 50 guns, length 146 ft., breadth 40 ft. 6 in., depth 17 ft. 6 in., tonnage 1,044. Laid down at Sheerness Yard in 1767, launched in 1770, sold in 1807.
The complement of men was 350.
Drawn by Josh. Williams, painted by Josh. Marshall, 1774.
Presented by Her Majesty.   1864.

12. Bow VIEW of H.M.S. "PORTLAND" (same ship as the preceding).
Drawn by J. Binmer, painted by Josh. Marshall, 1774.
Presented by Her Majesty.   1864.

13. STERN VIEW of H.M.S. "EXPERIMENT," 4th rate, 50 guns, length 140 ft. 9 in., breadth 38 ft. 8¼ in., depth 16 ft. 7 in., tonnage 923. Laid down at Messrs. Adams & Co.'s yard, on the Thames, in 1772, launched in 1774. Dismasted in a gale of wind, and taken the 22nd September 1779 by the French fleet, on her passage from New York to Savannah.
The complement of men was 300.
Drawn by Josh. Williams, painted by Josh. Marshall, 1775.
Presented by Her Majesty. 1864.

14. BOW VIEW of H.M.S. "EXPERIMENT" (same ship as the preceding).
Drawn by J. Binmer, painted by Josh. Marshall, 1775.
Presented by Her Majesty. 1864.

15. STERN VIEW of H.M.S. "AMBUSCADE," 5th rate, 32 guns, length 126 ft. 3 in., breadth 35 ft. 1¾ in., depth 12 ft. 2 in., tonnage 684. Laid down at Messrs. Adams & Co.'s yard, on River Thames in 1771, launched in 1773. Taken by the "BAYONAISE" in December 1798, afterwards retaken and broken up in 1813.
The complement of men was 220.
Drawn by Josh. Williams, painted by Josh. Marshall, 1775.
Presented by Her Majesty. 1864.

16. BOW VIEW of H.M.S. "AMBUSCADE" (same ship as the preceding).
Drawn by J. Binmer, painted by Josh. Marshall.
Presented by Her Majesty. 1864.

17. STERN VIEW of H.M.S. "ENTERPRIZE," 6th rate, 28 guns, length 120 ft. 6 in., breadth 33 ft. 6 in., depth 11 ft., tonnage 594. Laid down at Deptford Yard in 1771, launched in 1774, broken up in 1807.
The complement of men was 200.
Drawn by Josh. Williams, painted by Josh. Marshall, 1775.
Presented by Her Majesty. 1864.

18. BOW VIEW of H.M.S. "ENTERPRIZE" (same ship as the preceding).
Drawn by J. Binmer, painted by Josh. Marshall, 1775.
Presented by Her Majesty. 1864.

19. STERN VIEW of H.M.S. "SPHINX," 6th rate, 20 guns, length 108 ft., breadth 30 ft., depth 9 ft. 8 in., tonnage 429. Laid down at Portsmouth Yard in 1773, launched in 1775. Taken by the French in 1779, and retaken in December 1779 by the "PROSERPINE." Broken up at Portsmouth in 1811.

The complement of men was 160.
Drawn by Josh. Williams, painted by Josh. Marshall 1775.
Presented by Her Majesty.   1864.

20. BOW VIEW of H.M.S. "SPHINX" (same ship as the preceding).
Drawn by J. Binmer, painted by Josh. Marshall, 1775.
Presented by Her Majesty.   1864.

21. STERN VIEW of H.M.S. "KINGFISHER," sloop, 14 guns, length 96 ft. 8½ in., breadth 26 ft. 10 in., depth 12 ft. 10 in., tonnage 302. Laid down at Chatham Yard in 1769, launched in 1770, burnt at Rhode Island, 30th July 1778.

The complement of men was 125.
Drawn by Josh. Williams, painted by Josh. Marshall, 1775.
Presented by Her Majesty.   1864.

22. BOW VIEW of H.M.S. "KINGFISHER" (same ship as preceding).
Drawn by J. Binmer, painted by Josh. Marshall, 1775.
Presented by Her Majesty.   1864.

23. Two PAINTINGS of ships on copper. These paintings were used in the Royal Nursery, for the instruction of Prince William Henry, afterwards King William IV.
Presented by Mr. F. A. B. Bonney.   1865.

24. Two OIL PAINTINGS of the "GREAT BRITAIN," at "Low water" and "High water," by J. Walter, 1847.
Lent by Capt. Claxton, R.N.   1865.

Note.—The "GREAT BRITAIN," 3,600 tons. Iron screw steamer, built at Bristol, July 1843, from designs by I. K. Brunel; ran ashore in Dundrum Bay, Ireland, in September 1846, was exposed 11 months, and nearly submerged at every high tide; the sea in south-westerly and southerly gales making a clear breach all over her.

The breakwater here represented, combined with the "GREAT BRITAIN'S" admirable build, saved the vessel. The design for the breakwater was Brunel's, it consisted of 8,000 large faggots, 3 ft. in diameter and 12 or 13 ft. long, placed about the stern and exposed quarter, loaded with stones, and backed by two rows of .birch trees, about 60 ft. long. Brunel also designed the engines of the ship, and the gearing to drive the screw. The " GREAT BRITAIN " was got off by Capt. Claxton, R.N., in 1847–8.

25. BATTLE OF LEPANTO, Oct. 7, 1571. The great naval engagement between the combined fleets of Spain, Venice, Genoa, Malta, and Pius V. ; and the whole maritime force of the Turks. By Bonaventura Peters.
Lent by Mr. T. Dyer Edwardes.   1865.

26. BATTLE OF SOLEBAY, May 28, 1672, fought between the fleets of England and France on one side, and the Dutch on the other, the former commanded by the Duke of York, afterwards James II.
Lent by Mr. T. Dyer Edwardes.   1865.

27. BATTLE OF THE DOGGERBANK, in 1781, between the English and Dutch fleets. By T. Luny. 1781.
Lent by Mr. T. Dyer Edwardes.   1865.

28. MEN-OF-WAR IN PORT, by Anderson (b. 1757, d. 1837).
Lent by Mr. T. Dyer Edwardes.   1865.

29. SHIPPING, by Wimont. Painting.
Lent by Mr. T. Dyer Edwardes.   1865.

30. MALTESE GALLEY. Painting.
Lent by Mr. T. Dyer Edwardes.   1865.

31. OIL PAINTING of a Dutch man-of-war. By A. Stork.
Lent by Mr. T. Dyer Edwardes.   1868.

32. OIL PAINTING of an action between Maltese and Algerine vessels. By Vanvitelli, 1647–1736.
Lent by Mr. T. Dyer Edwardes.   1868.

33. OIL PAINTING of Maltese men-of-war at anchor. By Vanvitelli, 1647–1736.
Lent by Mr. T. Dyer Edwardes.   1868.

34. PICTURE of Dutch men-of-war. By Johannes Coesermans.
Lent by Mr. T. Dyer Edwardes.   1868.

35. OIL PAINTING of Dutch shipping. By Van Ass.
Lent by Mr. T. Dyer Edwardes.   1868.

See also series of Engravings, No. 60, page 128.

36. PAINTING IN OIL. A launch at Deptford Dockyard
English, middle of the 18th centy. By J. Cleveley.
Bought. Science and Art Department.   1867.

37. The American packet ship "WARREN" under jury
masts and temporary rudder. These were fitted after her
own had been carried away by a storm in the Mid-Atlantic,
and enabled her to reach England in safety.
Painted by Mr. George Mears.   1868.

38. PENCIL DRAWING of the hull of a man-of-war,
"SOVEREIGN OF THE SEAS," by William Van de Velde
(b. 1663, at Amsterdam, d. 1707).
Presented by Mr. George Smith.   1865.

39. A DRAWING of the port disposition of the frame of
H.M.S. "AMETHYST," wrecked in Bovesand Bay, Plymouth
Sound, in 1811. Her top side timbers had been continuously bolted, when last repaired according to the plan
proposed by the late "Joseph Tucker," Esq., Surveyor of
the Navy, and after having been 21 days on the rocks
during a gale of wind, she was floated off to Plymouth
Dockyard, with unbroken sheer.
Presented by Mr. John Scott Tucker.   1865.

40. DRAWING of a proposed 4-decked ship, the "DUKE
OF KENT," 170 guns, planned and proposed in 1809 by the
late "Joseph Tucker," Esq., Surveyor of the Navy, 1813–
1831.
Presented by Mr. John Scott Tucker.   1865.

The drawing shows lines, draught, profile, stern elevation,
&c. See Model, No. 4, Class I., p. 8.

DRAWINGS, &c. The following (15), lent (1868) by
Mr. John Scott Russell, F.R.S., are all of ships built by
him.

42. LONGITUDINAL DRAWING of the "GREAT EASTERN,"
steamship. Built 1857.   Lent, Mr. J. Scott Russell.

Note.—This drawing, on a scale of $\frac{1}{8}$ inch to 1 foot, gives a
longitudinal through section of the ship, showing the interior
arrangements throughout.

43. DRAWING, cross section of the "GREAT EASTERN"
steamship.   Lent, Mr. J. Scott Russell.

44. WATER-COLOUR DRAWING of the "GREAT EASTERN"
steamship, off the Isle of Wight. Lent, Mr. J. Scott Russell.

45. OIL PAINTING of the "GREAT EASTERN" steamship,
going through the Downs.   Lent, Mr. J. Scott Russell.

46. OIL PAINTING of the "GREAT EASTERN" steamship,
leaving the river Medway, off Sheerness.
                                              Lent, Mr. J. Scott Russell.

Note.—The "GREAT EASTERN" steamship was laid down
    in 1852, and launched in 1857, at Millwall. See model,
    Nos. 44, 45, 46, pp. 46, 47.

47. OIL PAINTING of the Royal West India Mail Company's fleet in Southampton Water.
                                              Lent, Mr. J. Scott Russell.

48. WATER-COLOUR DRAWING of the Sydney and Melbourne Royal Mail Steam Packet Company's paddle steamer
"PACIFIC," tons 1,470, horse-power 500.
                                              Lent, Mr. J. Scott Russell.

49. DRAWINGS of the Engines, Boilers, and Wheels of
the Sydney and Melbourne Royal Mail Steam Packet
Company's paddle-wheel steamer "PACIFIC," 500 horse-
power.
    See No. 15–8, p. 38.   Lent, Mr. J. Scott Russell.

50. WATER-COLOUR DRAWING of the Prussian man-of-
war paddle steamer, "DANTZIC;" guns 12 ; horse-power 400 ;
and Prussian frigates.   Lent, Mr. J. Scott Russell.

51. WATER-COLOUR DRAWING of the Prussian paddle
gun-boats "NIX" and "SALAMANDER."
                                              Lent, Mr. J. Scott Russell.

52. WATER-COLOUR DRAWING of "DANTZIC," "NIX,"
and "SALAMANDER," Prussian war ships, at gunnery practice.
                                              Lent, Mr. J. Scott Russell.

53. WATER-COLOUR DRAWING of a four-masted screw
steamer.   Lent, Mr. J. Scott Russell.

54. WATER-COLOUR DRAWING of a four-masted sailing
ship in a gale of wind.   Lent, Mr. J. Scott Russell.

55. WATER-COLOUR DRAWING of a screw steamer.
Lent, Mr. J. Scott Russell.

56. WATER-COLOUR DRAWING of the launch of a frigate at Millwall.   Lent, Mr. J. Scott Russell.

✱ The preceding 15 Drawings lent by Mr. John Scott Russell, F.R.S.   1868.

ENGRAVINGS AND DRAWINGS.

60. Series of ENGRAVINGS (23 in number) illustrating ships-of-war of early periods and of various countries.
Presented by Mr. T. Dyer Edwardes.   1868.
The principal engravings are—
An English second-rate ship-of-war of the smaller class. 1670.
A French second-rate. 1670.
A Spanish second-rate. 1670.
A Dutch second-rate. 1670.
The English fleet. 1342.
A Dutch ship-of-war.
Three English vessels. ships-of-war: The "GREAT "HARRY," 1503; the "ROYAL JAMES;" the "ROYAL "GEORGE," 1756.
A wicker boat of the ancient Britons.
The English war ship "HENRI GRACE À DIEU," 1520. 1,000 tons burthen.
The other engravings represent ships of ancient Rome, Maltese and Italian galleys, fire ships, &c.
See also Oil Paintings, No. 25 to 35, p. 125, 126.
Presented by Mr. T. Dyer Edwardes.   1868.

COLOURED CHART. British flags.
Presented by Mr. James Reynolds.   1864.

61. CHART, partly coloured, illustrating the Flags of all nations, the rigging and sails of a ship, and varieties of shipping.
Presented by Mr. James Reynolds.   1864.

62. ENGRAVINGS of "Lumley's" rudder, showing its modifications.
Lent by Mr. H. Lumley, Assoc. I.N.A.   1865.

63. COLOURED ENGRAVINGS of Capt. E. Bedford's, R.N., uniform code for the distinction of buoys by colour.
Presented by Capt. E. G. Bedford, R.N.   1867.

64. Two Engravings showing elevation, longitudinal section, &c. of improved life-boats, arranged to pack one in the other.

Presented by Mr. George Fawcus, North Shields.

1868

65. Drawings (lithographs).   59 Plates.

Lent by Mr. John Scott Russell, F.R.S., 1868, illustrating practical shipbuilding.

Plate 22.   Practical Ship Construction, Iron.
Midship section of an iron ship, showing internal construction and iron bulk-head.

Plate 33.   Projections.
Lines.   Paddle-wheel steamer.   Port view.

Plate 34.   Projections.
Lines.   Paddle-wheel steamer.   Starboard view.

Plate 35.   Projections.
Lines.   Paddle-wheel steamer.   Port view.

Plate 36.   Projections.
Lines.   Paddle-wheel steamer.   Starboard view.

Plate 37.   Projections.
Lines.   Screw steamer.

Plate 38.   Projections.
Lines.   Screw steamer.   Port view.

Plate 39.   Iron Shipbuilding.
The "Great Eastern" steamship.   Built 1857.   Lines.

Plate 40.   Iron Shipbuilding.
The " Great Eastern " steamship.   Built 1857.   Enlarged body plan.   Lines.

Plate 51.   Iron Shipbuilding.
The " Great Eastern " steamship.   Built 1857.   Iron deck plan.

Plate 57.   Lines and Structure.
Screw steam yacht, showing longitudinal sections, lines, deck plan, midship section, and sail draft.

Plate 58, 59.   Paddle-wheel steamships.
Royal steam yacht.
58, hull complete.   Upper deck plan.   Sail draft.
59, longitudinal through section.   Lower deck plan.

Plate 60, 61.   Paddle-wheel Steamships.
Extreme shallow-water navigation.
60, longitudinal through section and deck plan.
61, hull complete, and deck plan.

Plate 62.   Paddle-wheel steamships.
Channel mail packet.   Longitudinal through section.   Deck plan.

Plate 64.   Screw steamships.
Cargo trader, with water ballast hold.   Longitudinal through section.   Deck plan.

Plate 66. Screw steamships.
Screw collier. Longitudinal through section. Two deck plans.

Plate 67, 68. Paddle-wheel steamships.
Irish trader.
67, hull complete. Deck plan.
68, longitudinal through section. Deck plan.

Plate 69, 70. Paddle-wheel steamships.
Mediterranean trader and mail ship.
69, longitudinal through section.
70, two deck plans.

Plate 71, 72, 73, 74. Screw steamships.
Baltic trader and mail packet.
71, longitudinal through section.
72, upper deck plan.
73, under deck plan.
74, hull plan.

Plate 75. Screw steamships.
Auxiliary screw, China clipper. Longitudinal through section. Plan of iron deck.

Plate 83, 84. Ships of war.
Screw gun-boat.
83, hull, sail draft.
84, longitudinal section. Deck plan.

Plate 77, 78, 79. Screw steamships.
Australian passenger trader.
77, longitudinal through section.
78, upper deck plan.
79, passengers' cabins and saloon plan.

Plate 86, 87, 88. Ships of war, iron.
Paddle-wheel gunboat.
86, hull, drawing.
87, longitudinal through section.
88, deck plan.

Plate 94. Iron Shipbuilding.
The " GREAT EASTERN " steamship. Built 1857. External profile.

Plate 95. Iron Shipbuilding.
The " GREAT EASTERN " steamship, longitudinal through section.

Plate 96. Iron Shipbuilding.
The " GREAT EASTERN " steamship. First deck plan.

Plate 97. Iron Shipbuilding.
The " GREAT EASTERN " steamship. Second deck plan.

Plate 98. Iron Shipbuilding.
The " GREAT EASTERN " steamship. Third deck plan.

Plate 99. Iron Shipbuilding.
The " GREAT EASTERN " steamship. Fourth deck plan.

Plate 100. Iron Shipbuilding.
The " GREAT EASTERN " steamship. Fifth deck plan.

Plate 101. Iron Shipbuilding.
The " GREAT EASTERN " steamship. Built 1857. Cross section through paddle engine room.

Plate 102. Iron Shipbuilding.
The " GREAT EASTERN " steamship. Cross section through boiler room ; cross section through screw engine room.

Plate 103. Iron Shipbuilding.
The " GREAT EASTERN " steamship. Built 1857. Sail drafts, sections.

Plate 104. Iron Shipbuilding.
The " GREAT EASTERN " steamship. Sail draft ; half plan, upper deck, disposition of boats, cranes, &c.

Plate 105. Iron Shipbuilding.
The " GREAT EASTERN " steamship. Built 1857. Launching.

Plate 112. Wave-line Principles.
Forms of least resistance.

Plate 113. Wave-line Principles.
Pure wave-lines, body plan, profile, water lines, profile of stern on the vertical system, stern water-line, body stern plan, combined stern body plan.

Plate 114. Wave-line Principles.
1. Reconciled wave-lines, pure wave-line frame, double bow, profile water-lines, body plan.
2. Reconciled stern with pure wave-line form bow, water-lines, body plan.
3. Reconciled bow with reconciled stern, profile, water-lines, body plan.

Plate 115. Wave line Principles.
Compromised wave-lines, bow and stern forms, water-lines, body plans.

Plate 120. Paddle-wheel steamships. Iron.
Pacific royal mail ships.
Lines. Longitudinal through section.

Plate 123, 124. Paddle-wheel steamships. Iron.
Holyhead Royal Irish mail.
123. Longitudinal through section, upper deck plan.
124. Two deck plans, hold plan.

Plate 127. Paddle-wheel steamships. Iron.
French mail Brazilian liners.
Longitudinal through section. Two deck plans.

Plate 133. Ocean passenger and cargo ships.
Screw steamships. Iron.
Longitudinal through section. Two deck plans.

Plate 144. Ships of war. Iron armour ships.
Captain Cowper Coles' cupola ship.
   Fig. 1–4. Plans of arrangement for cupolas and deck.
   Fig. 5. Elevation, sail draft.
   Fig. 6. Midship section, sail draft.
Plate 145. Ships of war. Iron armour.
Captain Cowper Coles' cupola ship. (Gun turrets.)
   Figs. 1 and 3. Cross sections of turrets.
   Fig. 6. Elevation of turret.
   Figs. 2 and 4. Interior plans of turret.
   Fig. 7. Exterior plan, turret.
Plate.—Lloyd's Register of British and foreign shipping :—
   Illustrations of its rules for building iron ships, 1863 ; show-
   ing keelsons, side elevation, midship framings, beams, deck
   plans.

   *** The foregoing 59 plates, illustrating practical ship-
building, lent by Mr. John Scott Russell, F.R.S.   1868.

   67. Lithograph. Plans and sections of life-boat " Lady
Daly," built in Australia. Length 43 ft. 1 in., breadth
9 ft., depth midships 4 ft. 1 in. Designed by W. Taylor,
Government Shipwright, Port Adelaide, South Australia.
—About 1867.
     Lent by H.R.H. The Duke of Edinburgh.   1869.
     See Model of boat " Lady Daly," No. 1, p. 83.

   68. Drawing of the Pacific Steam Navigation Company's
Royal Mail screw steamship " Britannia."
Designed, engined, and built, by Messrs. Laird Brothers,
Birkenhead, 1873.
     Profile.—Sail draft, longitudinal section.
     Plans of spar, main, and lower decks.
     Engine and boiler rooms.
     Length 399 ft., breadth 43 ft., depth 35 ft. 3 in.
     Tons, o.m. 3,670. Horse-power 600. Has accommo-
     dation for 748 passengers.
     Lent by Messrs. Laird Brothers, Shipbuilders, Birken-
       head.   1874.
     See also Model of ship, Class I., No. 19, p. 12.

   69. Two Coloured Engravings of the screw steamship
" Archimedes " at sea, on 14th May 1839. Built in 1839
by Mr. H. Wimshurst, of Limehouse, for " The Ship Propeller Company."
   The ship fitted with Mr. Francis Pettit Smith's screw
propeller.
   Dimensions of ship " Archimedes " were :—
     Extreme length, 125 ft. ; extreme breadth, 22 ft. 6 in. ;
     depth, 13 ft. ; tons, 240 ; draught of water, 10 feet
     aft, 9 feet forward.

The engines were of 80 horse-power.

Diameter of screw, 5 ft. 9 in.; length of screw, 5 feet.

Screw was driven by vertical engines and multiplied wheel gearing.

The drawings show also profile of the ship.

Lent by Mr. Henry Wimshurst, Anerley Road.   1873.

See No. 12, p. 36.

70. LITHOGRAPH, illustrating methods of raising sunken ships and wrecks, by means of Messrs. Siebe, Gorman, and Christy's patent ship-raising iron pontoon.

Messrs. Siebe and Gorman, Submarine Engineers, Denmark Street, Soho.

Presented by Messrs. T. Christy & Co., 155, Fenchurch Street, E.C.   1873.

71. LITHOGRAPH.   Longitudinal elevation and cross sections illustrating Captain Archibald Thomson's proposals for the improved construction of screw steam ships.

See also Model, No. 43, p. 46.

Lent by Mr. A. Thomson.   1874.

72. DRAWING.   Pen and ink.   Port and starboard view of the figure-head of H.M.S. "WINDSOR CASTLE." Drawn by Mr. Nicholas Rundell, 1840.

Presented by Mr. J. B. Rundell.   1874.

73. PICTURE of the "RAINBOW," 1837.   Iron paddle steamer.   Length 185 ft., breadth 25 ft., depth 11 ft. 9 ins. 581 tons.   180 horse power.

Lent by Messrs. Laird Brothers, Engineers and Shipbuilders, Birkenhead.   1876.

Note.—The paddle steamer "RAINBOW" for passenger and cargo service was built for the General Steam Navigation Company of London, for service between London and Ramsgate.   After being employed in London and Antwerp trade for some time, the "RAINBOW," which was the fastest vessel of her day, ran for many years as a cargo steamer between Havre and London, and was in service till 1869.

She was fitted with a pair of upright engines known as "Steeple" engines, at one time greatly used for paddle-wheel steamships.

74. PICTURE of the ferry steamer "NUN," 1844.   Paddle wheel.   Length 105 ft., breadth 20 ft., depth 8 ft. 9 ins. 187 tons.   60 horse power.

Lent by Messrs. Laird Brothers, Engineers, and Shipbuilders, Birkenhead, 1876.

Note.—The picture shows the "NUN" grounded on the stone pier at Birkenhead, her after end resting on the pier,

and her bow on the bare rock below, the distance between
the points of support being 81 ft.; the whole weight of the
machinery, 65 tons, being in the middle of this unsupported
space. She floated off the succeeding tide without having
received the slightest damage.

This incident, which occurred in 1842, went far to confirm
the growing confidence in the strength of iron ships.

75. THREE DIAGRAMS of new type of war ships, designed
by Michael Scott in 1870, and published in 1871.

Lent by Mr. Michael Scott, F.R.S.E., London..
1876.

Note.—In this design there is a central fort, armour plated
all round ; an armoured deck under water sloping downwards
towards the bow, so as to prevent the vessel from being
raked in a seaway, and strengthening the ramming beak.
The ship is intended to carry sail, her turrets to be placed
abreast and also to carry broadside guns.

Some of the most important features in these designs have
been adopted in the most modern war ships.

76. THREE DIAGRAMS of a new type of war ship, designed
by Michael Scott in 1869, and published in 1870.

Lent by Mr. Michael Scott, F.R.S.E., London.
1876.

Note.—In this design the surface exposed to hostile fire is
diminished by constructing the vessel with a central fort,
armour plated all round, an armoured deck under water,
and dividing the space above this armoured deck for a height
of six feet into water-tight compartments, which would be
filled with fuel or water when going into action. She is
intended to carry both turret and broadside guns, and might
be armed with a submarine weapon.

77. DRAWING on cloth, for lecture purposes. Steamboat
designed in 1737 by Jonathan Hull, Engineer.

Lent by Mr. F. J. Bramwell, F.R.S.   1877.

Note.—Jonathan Hull claimed for his steamboat the power
of moving against tide and wind, and of towing against them
ships-of-war and other large vessels. There is an old work
published, with an engraving of this steamboat at work, and
the drawing is a copy of the engraving.

COLOURED DRAWINGS.

80. DRAWINGS of racing and pleasure boats, built by
Messrs. Searle & Sons, Stangate, Lambeth.

See also Nos. 2, 23, 24, Class IX., and Nos. 4, 4a, p. 103.

Lent.   1873.

Single sculling outrigger gig.
Length, 24 ft, Breadth, 2 ft. 8 in.

Sailing canoe.
Length, 14 ft.   Breadth, 2 ft. 8 in.

Four-oared gig with raised chocks.
Length, 24 ft.   Breadth, 3 ft. 5 in.

Four-oared outrigger gig.
Length, 38 ft.   Breadth, 2 ft. 5 in.

Lake boat, sailing or rowing.
Length, 20 ft.   Breadth, 4 ft. 9 in.

Dinghee.
Length, 12 ft.   Breadth, 4 ft. 6 in.

Eight-oared racing outrigger.
Length, 57 ft.   Breadth, 2 ft. 2 in.

Four-oared racing outrigger.
Length, 42ft.   Breadth, 1 ft. 9 in.

Pair-oared racing outrigger.
Length, 35 ft.   Breadth, 1 ft. 5 in.

Single sculling skiff.
Length, 22 ft.   Breadth, 3 ft. 6 in.

Pair-oared or double sculling gig.
Length, 26 ft.   Breadth, 3 ft. 10 in.

Sailing canoe.
Length, 15 ft.   Breadth, 3 ft. 2 in.

Pair-oared or double sculling gig.
Length, 24 ft.   Breadth, 3 ft. 8 in.

Pair-oared or double sculling gig.
Length, 24 ft.   Breadth, 3 ft. 8 in.

Randan skiff.
Length, 27 ft.   Breadth, 4 ft. 6 in.

Pair-oared skiff.
Length, 20 ft.   Breadth, 4 ft. 6 in.

Racing outrigger, with sliding seat.
Length, 32 ft.   Breadth, 1 ft.

Pair-oared or double sculling outrigger gig.
Length, 28 ft.   Breadth, 2 ft. 6 in.

Sailing gig, with centre board.
Length, 20 ft.   Breadth, 4 ft. 6 in.

Four-oared gig.
Length, 35 ft.   Breadth, 3 ft. 5 in.

Four-oared gig.
Length, 35 ft.   Breadth, 4 ft. 6 in.

Rob Roy canoe.
Length, 14 ft.   Breadth, 2 ft. 2 in.

Single sculling gig.
Length, 18 ft.   Breadth, 3 ft. 6 in.

Lent by Messrs. Searle & Sons, Lambeth. 1873.

₊ These drawings of boats are exhibited in one frame, glazed.

81. Two Coloured Drawings of the first screw steam-ship " Archimedes " on her voyage from London to Portsmouth in May 1839.

Presented to the late Vice-Admiral E. P. Halsted, R.N., and by him bequeathed to Museum.

These drawings will be found in the case of Ship Models presented by Messrs. R. Napier & Sons, Glasgow, in 1867.

See pages 8, 23, 83, 101.

82. Coloured Engraving (Lithograph) of the Admiralty Department Buildings, Whitehall, in 1808.

Published by Ackermann & Co., Strand.

· Presented 1876.

PHOTOGRAPHS.

84. Photograph of the fore topsail of Lord Nelson's ship " Victory," after the battle of Trafalgar in 1805.

Presented by Mr. S. Willcocks, Master Sailmaker, H.M. Dockyard, Sheerness.   1868.

85. Six Photographs, presented, 1869, by Messrs. R. Napier and Sons, Glasgow, of ships built by them, as follows :—

1. H.M.'s iron screw troopship "Malabar." Built and engined, 1867, by R. Napier & Sons. Length, 360 ft. ; breadth, 49 ft. ; depth, 22 ft. 4 in. ; tonnage, 4,173 ; horse-power, 700. See Model of H.M.'s ship "Jumna," Class I., p. 11.

2. Armour-clad monitor "De Tijger." Built, 1868, by R. Napier & Sons, for the Royal Dutch Government. Length, 187 ft.; breadth, 44 ft. ; depth, 11 ft. 6 in. ; tonnage, 1,612 ; horse-power, 140.

3. Armour-clad monitor "De Buffel." Built 1868, by R. Napier & Sons, for the Royal Dutch Government. Length, 205 ft.; breadth, 40 ft. ; depth, 24 ft.; tonnage, 1,472 ; horse-power, 400 ; twin screw.

4. Iron-clad screw frigates " Osman," " Ghazy," and Others on same lines. Built, 1866, by R. Napier & Sons, for the Imperial Ottoman Government. Tonnage, 4,221 ; horse-power, 900.

5. Screw steamships "Pereire " and "Ville de Paris." Built 1866, by R. Napier & Sons, for the French " Compagnie Générale Transatlantique." Length, 357 ft. ; breadth, 44 ft. ; depth, 29 ft.; tonnage,   ; horse-power, 800 ; speed, 15 knots.

6. Steam screw yacht, schooner rigged, " Vaynol." Tons, B.M. 48 ; horse-power, 20. Built by R. Napier & Sons, 1868.

86. PHOTOGRAPH of the screw steamship "CITY OF NEW YORK" leaving the River Mersey on her voyage to New York. Built, 1866, by Tod and McGregor, Glasgow. J. Walters, Liverpool, photo., 1867.

87. PHOTOGRAPH of the screw steamship "ORION," showing the effect of a collision with another vessel, off Beachy Head, December 21, 1869. Repaired by the London Engineering and Iron Shipbuilding Company (late Westwood, Baillie, and Co.), Isle of Dogs, Poplar, 1870.

Presented by Captain Symonds, R.N. 1870.

88. Set of PHOTOGRAPHS (four in number).

Two, of R. R. Bevis' patent feathering form inboard screw propeller, fitted to screw steam yacht "KATHLEEN," by Laird Brothers.

Two Photographs of the same screw propeller, showing plan and section.

Lent by Messrs. Laird Brothers, Birkenhead. 1873.

89. PHOTOGRAPH of the Whole Model lent by H.I.H. the Prince Napoleon in 1872 of the Imperial French screw steam yacht "JEROME NAPOLEON." 1873.

90. Series of DRAWINGS and PHOTOGRAPHS illustrating the following marine steam engines and boilers, steam winches, and fresh-water distilling apparatus.

Messrs. Alexander Chaplin and Co., Glasgow.

Photograph of a twin screw vertical steam engine and boiler.

Photograph of a double cylinder screw engine with horizontal steam boiler.

Photograph of a double cylinder paddle-boat engine with vertical boiler.

Drawing on a 1 inch to 1 foot scale of steamships' winding engine, with distilling apparatus for fresh water, and steam cooking hearth.

Drawing on 6 inches to 1 foot scale of an improved donkey steam engine for feeding steam boilers with water.

Drawing on 1½ inch to 1 foot scale of a ship's improved steam winch.

The above six drawings and photographs of ships' steam apparatus presented by Messrs. Alexander Chaplin and Co., Glasgow. 1874.

See also No. 13, page 140.

91. PHOTOGRAPH of the "COMET" and "IONA" steamers, 1811, 1874.

Lent by Mr. John Hamilton, Glasgow.   1876.

Note. — From a painting by Wm. Clark-Greenock, to illustrate and keep on record the appearance of the first British steamer, and also to make a comparison between the past and present types of Clyde river steamers.

CLASS XVI.

Miscellaneous Objects and Models not comprised in the foregoing Classes.

1. MODEL of the JETTY, and SHEERS for masting-ships. Sheerness Dockyard. . 1864.

2. Set of TELESCOPES formerly belonging to, and used by, Admiral Lord Nelson.

> Lent by Mr. W. H. Maitland. 1869.
> The set consists of, one 4 ft. glass; one day and night glass; one hand glass; two spare tubes, and an eye piece.

3. CAP worn by sailors on board the "INFERNAL," bomb ketch. Commanded by the Hon. Capt. Perceval (Lord Egmont), at the siege of Algiers, in 1816.

> Presented by Sir W. Trevelyan, Bart. 1869.

4. FIGURE HEAD for a ship. Full size. Coloured.

> Lent by late Mr. R. Hall, 1865, now Messrs. Culmore & Long, Rotherhithe. 1874.

5. WOODEN FIGURE HEAD of a native Canoe, New Zealand. Carved in hard wood and painted red.

> Presented by Mr. R. H. Rhodes. 1876.

6. ORNAMENTAL CARVED WORK, in wood, for bow and stern of ships, proposed for H.M.'s ships of the "ROYAL OAK" class; by Mr. Hellyer, carver to the Admiralty. 1860. 1864.

7. Two smooth-boring AUGER BITS. Recommended by the late Mr. Joseph Tucker, Joint Surveyor of H.M. Navy from 1813 to 1831, for the reduction of decay in wooden ships.

> Presented by Mr. J. S. Tucker. 1865.

8. MODEL. Machine for rolling bars of metal for bolts, &c.

> Designed by Sir Robert Seppings, 1829. 1864.

9. Two specimens of IRON BOILER PLATE; (A) atlas iron plate; (B) best iron plate for boilers.

> From the Atlas Steel and Iron Works, Sheffield. 1864.

10. Piece of BOILER SCALE, from the steam boiler of a land engine. The specimen (polished) clearly shows the formation, and defines the adhesion to the boiler plates.
> Presented by the Institution of Naval Architects, per Mr. Merrifield.   1871.

11. Two BEARINGS for shafts or axles fitted with white metal ; they have been in use on the Great Western Railway.
> Messrs. J. Woods & Co.   1864.

12. WORKING MODEL of a steam pile Driving Engine for submarine foundations and other work. Sissons & White's patent.
> Lent by Messrs. Sissons & White, Hull.   1869.

Note.—This Model, on about ½-inch scale, is a complete working illustration of a steam pile driver. The crane to raise the monkey by an endless chain is driven by frictional gearing by the engine, which represents a high pressure inverted cylinder direct acting engine, having slide valve, eccentric, fly-wheel, and force pump for feeding the boiler with water. The boiler represents an upright tubular boiler for working at high pressure.

13. Series of DRAWINGS and PHOTOGRAPHS illustrating Steam Machinery manufactured by Messrs. Alexander Chaplin and Co., Glasgow.
> Photograph of a steam winding and pumping engine.
> Photograph of a steam crane.
> Photograph of a single cylinder hoisting engine.
> Photograph of a winding and pumping engine.
> Photograph of a contractor's locomotive engine.
> Drawing on a 1½ inches to 1 foot scale of Messrs. Chaplin and Co.'s patent vertical steam boiler.
> Photograph of a travelling fresh-water distilling apparatus.
> The above seven drawings and photographs presented by Messrs. Alexander Chaplin and Co., Glasgow.   1874.
> See also No. 90, page 137.

14. DRAWING of Richardson's patent vertical steam Boiler. Robey and Co., makers.
> Lent by Messrs. Robey and Co., Lincoln.   1874.

15. DRAWING of a patent tubular upright steam Boiler called the " Nozzle boiler," designed and made by the Reading Ironworks Co., Limited, Reading. A 4 horse-power horizontal high-pressure steam engine.
> Lent by the Reading Ironworks Co., Limited. 1874.

NOTE.—*Illustrations Nos. 12, 13, 14, 15, being steam machinery applicable to work in connexion with the excavation and erection of harbours, docks, quays, &c., have a place in the Catalogue and Collection.*

16. Sectional Model, showing 10th of the length of the Iron Floating Docks at the Royal Spanish Arsenal Carthagena and Ferrol, Spain.   Built 1856–57.
Lent by J. and G. Rennie, Engineers, Blackfriars.
1876.

Note.—The model (in wood) represents the interior and exterior of these floating docks built by Messrs. Rennie for the Spanish Government, and within the model a $\frac{1}{10}$th portion of an iron armour plated ship of war of a total weight of 6,500 tons.

The dock measures 350 feet total length ; 105 feet extreme breadth ; 37 feet 6 inches inside depth.

Displacement of base 13,000 tons.   Total weight of dock complete 6,500.

This model is on a scale of 1 inch to 1 foot, and shows the arrangements on the top sides, in the bottom, and other detail.

17. Whole Model of an iron Floating Dock.   Built by Messrs. Randolph, Elder, & Co., Glasgow ; for Port Saigon, Cochin China.   For the French Government.
Lent by Messrs. John Elder and Co., Govan, near Glasgow.   1876.

Note.—The dimensions of this iron floating dock are :—

Length extreme	-	-· 300 ft.
Breadth „	-	- 94 ft.
Depth „	-	- 42 ft.

The dock will lift a ship of 4,800 tons weight, drawing 27 feet of water.   The weight of the dock is 2,800 tons.

18. Photographs of Campbell's Patent Floating Dry Dock constructed of iron, for Her Majesty's Dockyard, Bermuda, 1868.   Length extreme 381 feet, length inside 330 feet.   Width extreme 123 ft. 1 inch, width inside 83 feet, 1 inch.   Height extreme 74 feet 5 inches, height inside 54 ft. 5 in.
Lent by Messrs. Campbell, Johnstone, & Co., Founders Court, Lothbury, E.C.   1876.

Note.—This iron floating dock for Bermuda was built by Messrs. Campbell, Johnstone & Co., at Silvertown, North Woolwich ; and launched broadside on in September 1868. There are 3 photographs of this floating dock.   One represents the dock before launching ; a second represents the dock heeled over at Bermuda for cleaning.   The third represents this dock carrying H.M.'s armour plated ship "Royal Alfred."

The Bermuda Floating Dock will sustain ships of war of H.M.S. "Fury" class, iron armour plated ship of 10,000 tons burthen.

19. PHOTOGRAPH of the Floating Iron Dock at Bermuda; carrying H.M.'s armour plated ship "ROYAL ALFRED," 4068 tons, 800 horse-power, nominal.

Lent by Messrs. Campbell, Johnstone, & Co., Founders Court, Lothbury, E.C.   1876.

Note.—The extreme length of this dock is 381 feet. Length between caisons 330 feet. The extreme width 123 feet, 9 inches. Inside width, 83 feet, 1 inch. Extreme height 74 feet, 5 inches. Inside height 54 feet, 5 inches. The dock was finished and towed out to Bermuda in 1869. See also No. 18, p. 141.

---

20. FIRST HELMET made for Diving Purposes, date A.D. 1829.

Lent by Messrs. Siebe and Gorman, Denmark Street, Soho.   1876.

21. PATENT HELMET for Diving, fitted with segmental neck ring and safety locking arrangement, inflating valve for bringing diver to the surface. Fitted with speaking apparatus to enable the diver to communicate with his attendant. Used on board H.M. Ships of the Royal Navy.

Lent by Messrs. Siebe and Gorman, Denmark Street, Soho.   1876.

22. Sectional MODEL of a Diving Bell for sub-marine explorations. The Model illustrates an arrangement by Dr. John Taylor, for supplying air to the bell in an upward jet near the mouth ; so that in case of the bursting of the air hose or the failure of the stop-valve (usually placed on the top of the bell) the water would only rise to the level of the air-pipe nozzle.

Presented by the late Dr. John Taylor, M.D., Professor of Natural Philosophy, in the Andersonian University, Glasgow.   1874.

23. MODEL illustrating Mr. H. S. Harland's proposed Apparatus for saving the lives of bathers and skaters on lakes and rivers, and showing the installation on the water side.

9 thread tarred cordage to be employed.

Presented by Mr. H. S. Harland, Brompton, Scarborough.   1874.

24. " BAILLIE," Weight Detaching Apparatus ; date 1872. By Navigating Lieut. C. W. Baillie, R.N.   In general use in H.M.S. "CHALLENGER." Scientific expedition, 1873–1876.

Lent by the Admiralty.   1876.

Note.—Iron sinkers of half a hundredweight each (exhibited in wood models) in numbers sufficient for varying ocean depths, are placed on the sounding tube and suspended by the ring and wire to two shoulders that project from the sides of a sliding rod working in the upper part of the sounding tube.   On touching sea bottom and the sounding line slackening, the sinker weights draw the sliding rod downwards, and the shoulders passing within the sounding tube, the wire is thrown off, and the weights released.   The lower portion of the tube, to which a valve is attached, receives the specimen of the sea bottom.

25. SPECIMENS of Sounding Line.   Used in H.M. ships. No. 1, used in " CHALLENGER," 1873–1876.   No. 2, medium.

Lent by the Admiralty.   1876.

Note.—These lines are constructed of the best Italian hemp.

No. 1 line is one inch in circumference ; 100 fathoms (or 600 feet) weighs 18 lbs. 9 oz.   When wet this line breaks at a minimum strain about 14 hundredweight.

No. 2 line is 0.8 inches in circumference ; 100 fathoms weighs 12 lbs. 8 oz., and it bears a strain of about 10 cwt. when wet.

26. WATER BOTTLE.   In ordinary use for bringing up water from ocean depths.   (Superseded in H.M. ship "CHALLENGER."   Scientific expedition, 1873–1876, by Buchanan's design.)   See No. 27.

Lent by the Admiralty.   1876.

27. WATER BOTTLE.   Buchanan's ; date 1872.   Invented by Mr. Buchanan, one of the scientific civilian staff attached to "CHALLENGER."   Scientific expedition, 1873–1876.

Lent by the Admiralty.   1876.

28. CUP LEAD.   For Sounding in depths not exceeding 1,000 fathoms, and to procure specimens of the sea bottom (about 1858).   Model.   Originally used in sounding North Atlantic.

Lent by the Admiralty.   1876.

29. TUBE LEAD. For Sounding in depths not exceeding 1,000 fathoms, and procuring specimens of the sea bottom ; date 1872. Model. In use in H.M.S. "CHALLENGER" Scientific expedition, 1873–1876.
Lent by the Admiralty.   1876.

30. TRAWL NETS, SIEVES, and other gear used on board H.M.S. "CHALLENGER" during her Scientific expedition round the world, 1873 to 1876.
Lent by the Admiralty.   1876.

31. MASSEY'S self-registering Sounding Machine. Date 1800. Adapted for moderate depths. In use in H.M. Navy.
Lent by the Admiralty.   1876.

32. DIAGRAMS and REGULATIONS illustrating the "Rule of the Road" at sea, for sailing and steamships.
By Mr. Thomas Gray, Board of Trade.   1872.

33. FISH TRAPS. Baskets for catching shrimps during the wet season. Used at Logos, West Coast of Africa.
From the London International Exhibition, 1874.
                                                         1875.

34. SPECIMENS of Fishing Nets used in French fisheries.
Presented by Mr. C. W. Merrifield, F.R.S.   1868.

35. Silver CLARET JUG and SALVER presented in 1858 by a company of gentlemen and engineers, to the late Sir Francis Pettit Smith, in recognition of his exertions in the application and development of the screw propeller for the propulsion of ships.
Bequeathed by the late Sir Francis Pettit Smith.
                                                         1871.

36. A PANTAMETER, No. 1 size. For indicating the specific gravity of iron, wood, and coal, the sectional area of bars, and the cubic contents of any body that will go into the machine.   Lent by Mr. A. M. Bennett. 1868.

APPENDIX.

Class I., No. **55.** WHOLE MODEL of an ocean going screw steamship designed for the service of the Eastern Telegraph Company by E. W. Briscoe.

E. W. Briscoe, 37 Gracechurch Street, E.

Lent. 1877.

Note.—This ocean-going ship was designed by Mr. Briscoe for the purpose of picking up and repairing ocean telegraph cables. Her principal dimensions are—length between perpendiculars 300 feet ; breadth of beam 40 feet; extreme depth from top of keel to underside of deck 20 feet. Tonnage O.M. 2349. The model is on a scale of ¼ inch to 1 foot.

Class I., No. **56.** WHOLE MODEL of a double-ended paddle steamer for Channel service from France to England. Designed by A. and J. Inglis, Point House, Ship Yard, Glasgow.

Lent. 1877.

Note.—The whole model represents a paddle steamer designed by A. and J. Inglis to meet the requirements of Mr. John Fowler's, C.E., and others Channel ferry scheme 1870. The steamer has an awning deck amidships, and is so constructed as to take on board a train of railway carriages at either end, and to carry mails and passengers across the English Channel.

Class I., No. **57.** WHOLE MODEL of an iron sailing ship designed by Mr. Gilbert Row, 31 Guildford Road, Greenwich.

Lent. 1877.

Note.—The model represents an iron sailing ship above 1,200 tons register. She is a clipper ship with full poop and topgallant forecastle, with extensive accommodation for first-class passengers, together with a large carrying capacity. The starboard side of the model shows horizontal longitudinal sections, and the port side shows vertical longitudinal sections. Her principal dimensions are—Length, over all, 220 feet 6 inches ; length of keel and fore rake 212 feet ; breadth, extreme, 37 feet ; depth of hold 22 feet 8 inches; load draught 19 feet 3 inches ; register tonnage N.N.M. 1,297 $\frac{97}{100}$ tons ; displacement at load line 2,599 $\frac{3}{4}$ tons.

K 2

Class I., No. **58.** WHOLE MODEL of an iron sailing ship about 1,800 tons register. Designed by Charles H. Jordan, 21 Circus Street, Greenwich.

Lent.   1877.

Class II., No. **48.** HALF BLOCK MODEL of the iron screw steamship " DEVONIA." Built 1876 by the Barrow Shipbuilding Company.

Lent by the Barrow Iron Shipbuilding Company, Barrow-in-Furness: 1877.

Note.—The screw steamer " DEVONIA " was built for the Anchor Line of steamships for passenger trade between Great Britain and America. Her length is 400 feet between perpendiculars. Tonnage 4,500. The ship was built and engined in 1877 by the Barrow Iron Shipbuilding Company, Barrow-in-Furness, and will eventually trade between the port of Barrow and New York.

Class II., No. **49.** HALF BLOCK MODEL of an iron passenger and cargo steamer for Atlantic trade.

Lent by Messrs. J. and G. Thomson, Clyde Bank . Foundry, Glasgow.   1877.

Note.—The model represents a proposed iron screw steamship for ocean service of the following dimensions : length 420 ft.; beam 45 ft. ; depth 35 ft.; tons, gross, 4,858. Horse power indicated 4,500. Designed 1877.

Class V., No. **16.** MODELS (2) of Patent Portable Anchors. Designed by Captain A. Thomas Swinburne, late R.N. Salen, Fort William, N.B.

Lent.   1877.

Class VII., No. **82.** Set of Patent Cups or Lubricators for marine engines. Page and East's patent.

Messrs. Page and East, Harrison's Wharf, St. Catherine's, E.   1877.

Note.—These oil cups are in use on board H.M. ships, and commercial steam vessels. They are self-acting and are said to have produced a saving of 35 per cent. in tallow or other lubricating matter, compared with grease cups of the ordinary form.

Class X., No. **30.** THREE SHIPS' LIGHTS. Full size. Port, starboard, and masthead lights.

Mr. William Harvie, 220, Broomielaw, Glasgow.

Lent.   1877.

Note.—These ships' lights are essentially different in arrangement, burners, and lenses to ordinary ships' lights; they have been tested at Shoeburyness with much success for night signalling purposes.

Class X., No. **31.** SET OF SHIPS' LIGHTS, port, starboard, and masthead lights.

Mr. C. E. Halls, 74, St. George's Street, E.
Lent.   1877.

Note.—These are fitted with Hall's patent prismatic-cut lenses for increasing the volume of light.

Class X., No. **32.** SET OF YACHTS' LIGHTS. Port, starboard, and masthead lights.

Mr. C. E. Halls, 74, St. George's Street, E.
Lent.   1877.

Note.—These are fitted with Hall's patent prismatic-cut lenses for increasing the volume of light. Besides these ships' lights are two masthead or riding lights, one full size for ships'use, and one smaller size for yachts.

Class X., No. **33.** SHIPS' COMPASS and BINNACLE, of BRASS. Fitted complete; with two lights.

Mr. C. E. Halls, 74, St. George's Street, E.
Lent.   1877.

Note.—The compass and binnacle exhibited represents the size and form chiefly used for yachts.

Class X., No. **34.** COMPASS and BINNACLE, of BRASS. Fitted complete for boats' use ; with one light.

Mr. C. E. Halls, 74, St. George's Street, E.
Lent.   1877.

Note.—This compass and binnacle is designed with a view to its immediate use in ships' boats. It can be shipped or unshipped aboard as wanted, in one minute.

Class XII., No. **16.** HALF BLOCK MODEL of a sea-going fishing smack. Designed by T. V. Trew, Barking.
Lent.   1877.

Note.—The model represents a smack of the following dimensions : length, on deck, extreme 67 ft. ; breadth 19 ft. ; depth 9 ft. 6 in. ; draft of water 9 ft.

Class XII., No. **17.** HALF BLOCK MODEL of a sea-going fishing smack. Designed and built by T. V. Trew, Barking.
Lent.   1877.

Note.—This model represents a fishing smack of the following dimensions : length, on deck, 63 ft. ; breadth, extreme 18 ft. 6 in. ; depth 11 ft. 3 in. ; draft of water 9 ft. 6 in.

Class XII., No. **18.** WHOLE MODEL of a sea-going sailing barge. A topsail barge, to carry 85 tons on a 5 ft. 6 in. draft of water. Designed by W. J. Talbot, Chiswick.

> Lent by W. J. Talbot, Strand-on-the-Green, Chiswick.   1877.

> *Note.*—The sailing barge represented by the model is designed for sailing at a good speed to carry a large cargo on a light draft. She is full rigged and fitted with gear in complete working order. There is also a working drawing of this barge, showing sheer, body plans, and water lines, longitudinal section, plan of deck, profiles of head and stern, midship section. The drawings are on a scale of $\frac{1}{4}$ in. to 1 foot. The model is on a scale of 1 in. to 1 foot.

Class XII., No. **19.** HALF BLOCK MODEL designed and built by Messrs. Watkins & Co. for a racing cutter yacht on clipper lines. The "BONITA." Tons 10.

> Lent by Messrs. Watkins & Co., Blackwall, E.   1877.

Class XII., No. **20.** HALF BLOCK MODEL designed and built by Messrs. Watkins & Co. for a yawl yacht on clipper lines. The "MERSEY." Hon. F. Stanley owner. Tons 40. 1875.

> Lent by Messrs. Watkins & Co., Blackwall, E.   1877.

Class XII., No. **21.** HALF BLOCK MODEL of the screw steam launch "JACKDAW," Captain R. Goff owner. Scale $\frac{1}{4}$ in. to 1 ft. Built by Messrs. Watkins & Co., Blackwall, E.

> Lent.   1877.

· Class XII., No **22.** HALF BLOCK MODEL of twin screw steam launch "SISCEEPE" Viscount Milton owner. Scale $\frac{1}{4}$ in. to 1 ft. Built by Messrs. Watkins & Co., Blackwall, E.

> Lent.   1877.

Class XII., No. **23.** HALF BLOCK MODEL of screw steam launch "FLY BY NIGHT." Messrs. Lough Brothers owners. Scale $\frac{1}{4}$ in. to 1 ft. Built by Messrs. Watkins and Co., Blackwall, E. Lent.   1877.

Class XII., No. **24.** HALF BLOCK MODEL of a river screw tug. Treble screw tug.

> Lent by Mr. George Scott, Govan, Glasgow.   1877.

> *Note.*—This treble screw tug, built of iron for river use, is fitted with a pair of screws (twin screws) at the stern and one screw at the bow in her fore foot. A system of double screw

tug boats fitted with a single screw forward and a single screw aft has been successfully carried out by Messrs. Howden and Co. of Glasgow.

Class XII., No. **25.** HALF BLOCK MODEL of a river screw tug. Designed and built by J. Stewart, Blackwall Works, Isle of Dogs, E.

Lent. 1877.

Class I., No. **59.** WHOLE MODEL of a wooden 36-gun frigate. About 1780. Scale ¼ inch to 1 foot.

Lent by Mrs. Hooper, 72, Petherton Road, Highbury New Park. 1877.

Note.—The model has poop and topgallant forcastle, and exhibits the whole of the ship's upper deck fittings and guns.

Class I., No. **60.** WHOLE MODEL rigged of a Revenue cutter. About 1810–30. Scale ¼ inch to 1 foot.

Lent by Mrs. Hooper, 72, Petherton Road, Highbury New Park. 1877.

Note.—This model is built and represents an old Revenue cutter of 14 guns. The detail of the upper deck fittings is complete. The rigging and gear of the cutter are carried out with extreme exactitude, and the little figures in the shrouds represent part of the vessel's crew.

Class XII., No. **26.** WHOLE MODEL of a modern cutter yacht rigged. Scale ½ inch to 1 foot.

Lent by Mrs. Hooper, 72, Petherton Road, Highbury New Park. 1877.

Note.—The detail of the rigging of this yacht is complete. The model represents a vessel of about 60 feet long by 12 feet beam.

Class XVI., No. **37.** MODEL representing formation and construction of a proposed deep-water harbour in Filey Bay, coast of Yorkshire. Designed about 1870 by Sir John Coode, C.E.

Lent by the Home Office. 1877.

Note.—The anchorage enclosed by the breakwater as shown on this model would be completely sheltered in all winds, and its total area at low water ordinary spring tides would equal 750 acres.

380 acres area would have a depth of 5 fathoms and upwards, 200 acres would have a depth of 6 fathoms, and 60 acres would have a depth of 7 fathoms of low water ordinary spring tides.

An additional area of nearly 1,200 acres would also be sheltered from northerly and easterly winds.

Class XVI., No. **38.** MODEL showing the operations and construction of one of the docks by Convict labour, at the new extension works, Chatham Dockyard. 1870. Scale of model :--For the area, 20 feet to 1 inch ; for the width of entrances to docks, 10 feet to 1 inch ; the basin, walls, men, horses, &c., 5 feet to 1 inch. The model was made by convicts at Chatham Prison.

Lent by the Home Office.   1877.

Note.—The addition to the Dockyard at Chatham (of which this model shows a small portion as it actually appeared under construction by Convict labour) covers a space of 430 acres, which is four times the extent of the old dockyard.

It occupies the site of St. Mary's Island, the original condition of which is shown by another model. The channel which separated the island from the mainland furnished the position of the basins. The bottom of the basins is 12 feet below the old river-bed, and 32 feet below St. Mary's Island. The island—which was formerly much intersected by creeks, and nearly covered at high water—has been raised about 8 feet by spreading on it the earth excavated out of the basins, &c. Convict labour was employed for the purpose. The whole island will be surrounded by a sea-wall and embankment, 9,200 feet or nearly two miles in length, the greater portion being executed by Convict labour.

There are three basins :—

1. The " Repairing Basin," covering 21 acres, in which ships are completed after being launched, or are repaired.

2. The " Factory Basin " (shown in the model), covering 20 acres, into which ships are taken to have their engines and boilers put into them. This basin was commenced by prisoners in June 1869, and finished in December 1871.

3. The " Fitting-out Basin," at which the prisoners are now at work, covering 28 acres. Ships will be rigged, and receive their guns, stores, and coals in this basin.

Total wet dock accommodation 69 acres.

The "Repairing Basin" is 700 feet wide, a width determined by the space necessary for the largest ship to turn in, when the wharves are occupied by other vessels. It has four docks, each 469½ feet long and 109 feet wide. These are capable of holding the largest ship ever contemplated for the Royal Navy, or any ship in the world, except the "GREAT EASTERN." The depth of water in the basin and docks is 36 feet at spring-tides.

The bricks for the whole of these works, nearly 117,000,000 in number up to date (1877), have been made by Convict labour, which has also executed the carpenters', blacksmiths', bricklayers', and other trades; necessary in the construction of the works.

The model contains the figures of 295 prisoners, 40 superior and subordinate officers, and 14 free-men; the last-named were formerly employed as engine drivers and stokers, but these duties also are now performed by prisoners. There were, however, a considerably larger number of prisoners at work in the construction of this basin than is shown on the model; and the daily average number of prisoners employed annually on the Admiralty works is 1,130.

Class X., No. **35.** INSTRUMENT and APPARATUS for determining at all times by electric or magnetic means, the latitude, longitude, and speed of a ship at sea. Designed and patented in 1876 by Tito Visino as a hydrograph.

Lent by Miss Clough, Park Lodge, King's Road, Clapham Park. 1877.

Note.—The Hydrograph is intended to trace by self-acting mechanism, on a kind of hydrographic map, the course of a vessel, and to register continuously and permanently her speed, movements, and position (latitude and longitude), at any moment by day or night. It consists of three parts. The first being a counting apparatus or log; the second an electro-magnetic needle to act in conjunction with the log; thirdly, a graphic apparatus governed by the log and the electro-magnetic needle, for recording on the hydrographic map the ship's course.

Class XVI., No. **37.** MODEL of Sheers for masting and fitting ships. Constructed by Messrs. Day, Summers, and Co., Southampton.

Lent 1876.

Note.—The sheers represented by the model have three hollow legs constructed of wrought-iron boiler plate, and are controlled and manœuvred by steam power.

152

ALPHABETICAL INDEX to SUBJECTS in the CATALOGUE of the COLLECTION of SHIP MODELS and MARINE ENGINEERING in the SOUTH KENSINGTON MUSEUM.

₊ *Objects in this Index not having a page reference are desiderata not yet in the collection.*

LONDON :

Printed by GEORGE E. EYRE and WILLIAM SPOTTISWOODE,
Printers to the Queen's most Excellent Majesty.
For Her Majesty's Stationery Office.
[10037.—500.—1/78.]

www.ingramcontent.com/pod-product-compliance
Lightning Source LLC
Chambersburg PA
CBHW021807190326
41518CB00007B/484